WORDS OF WELLNESS

WORDS OF WELLNESS

A Treasury of Quotations for
Well-Being

Compiled and Edited
by
Joseph Sutton

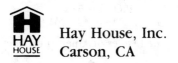

Hay House, Inc.
Carson, CA

WORDS OF WELLNESS
A Treasury of Quotations for Well-Being
Compiled and Edited by Joseph Sutton

Copyright © 1991 by Joseph Sutton

Library of Congress Catalog Card No. 90-71110
ISBN: 1-56170-005-3

Library of Congress Cataloging-in-Publication Data

Words of wellness : a treasury of quotations for well-being / compiled and edited by Joseph Sutton
    p.   cm.
    Includes bibliographical references.
    ISBN 1-56170-005-3 (trade : recycled paper) : $12.00
    1. Health—Quotations, maxims, etc. 2. Medicine—Quotations, maxims, etc. I. Sutton, Joseph, 1940–
RA776.5.W67   1991
613—dc20
                          90-71110
                          CIP

Internal design by John K. Vannucci
Typesetting by Freedmen's Typesetting Organization,
Los Angeles, CA 90004

91 92 93 94 95 96   10 9 8 7 6 5 4 3 2 1
First Printing, May 1991

Published and Distributed in the United States by

Hay House, Inc.
1154 E. Dominguez St.
P.O. Box 6204
Carson, CA 90749-6204 USA

Printed in the United States of America on Recycled Paper

Dedication

In memory of my mother, JEANETTE SUTTON,
who taught me the basics of health

Table of Contents

INTRODUCTION

I originally intended to gather health quotations on the mind and body and leave it at that. As I burrowed deeper into the subject of health, though, it dawned on me that not only were the mind and body intertwined, but along with them the spirit and emotions as well. Our health, I discovered, depends on every aspect of our lives. It depends on the work we do, our relationship with others, our self-image, our dreams and hopes, whether we exercise, what we eat and drink, how we think, the environment we live in, whether we laugh or get angry—all these things are somehow interconnected and have an equal bearing on our health. That's why the quotations in WORDS OF WELLNESS take into account the full spectrum—the mental, physical, spiritual and emotional facets—of our being.

I gleaned these quotations from the sages of all ages, from Confucius to Shakespeare to Mae West to Woody Allen. Some of the "sages" I've quoted are not so well known, while others are not known at all. We must remember, though, it's the words that count, not the person who said them.

I found in my research that no matter how far back we go in history we can find that what was said then is as up-to-date as what is said today. Cicero, who lived from 106-43 B.C., wrote: *"Exercise can preserve something of our early vigor even in old age."* The man who introduced the word "aerobics" to the English language in 1968, Dr. Kenneth H. Cooper, has written: *"Exercise is absolutely essential to good health. It's a major key to an energetic, long life."* This is one of many similarities of the past meeting the present in WORDS OF WELLNESS.

Each quotation is in one of 116 categories. The categories are alphabetized for easy access. For instance, if you have an interest in walking, like I do, you can turn to the *"Walking"* category. Of all the healing thoughts in this book, the one penned by George Macaulay Trevelyan is my favorite: *"I have two doctors, my left leg and my right. When body and mind are out of gear I know that I shall have only to call in my doctors and I shall be well again."* I was ecstatic when I came across this saying. It was something I had known intuitively for years but never expressed it. In fact, it was this quotation that planted the seed for what is now this book.

Let's say you're interested in cutting down on your food intake. There are a few categories in WORDS OF WELLNESS to motivate or inspire you to do just that. You can turn to the *"Eating/Diet"* category where you'll find a simple yet powerful Chinese proverb that goes: *"Everything you eat affects you profoundly."* In the *"Excess"* category there is a thought by Orson Welles, who said: *"Gluttony is not a secret vice."* Mr. Welles, an extremely robust and talented man in his day, truly knew what he was talking about when he came up with that gem. Or maybe leafing through the *"Moderation/Temperance"* category can keep you from overeating. One of my favorite quotes comes from John Heywood, who said: *"Enough is as good as a feast."*

We live in a world nowadays where practically everyone is in a great big huge monstrous rush. Some people are so harried and frazzled that the best thing for them to do would be to sit themselves down and read the complete *"Relaxation/Rest"* category. Lily Tomlin's words might hit the bull's-eye for them: *"For fast-acting relief, try slowing down."*

I personally find the quotations in this book both inspirational and informative. If I'm lax about exercising, if I'm depressed, if I'm worried too much about something, if I'm impatient with my 10-year-old son, I turn to this book and somehow it helps cure whatever ills I might have. As Thomas Carlyle once wrote: *"The best effect of any book is that it excites the reader to self-activity."* WORDS OF WELLNESS has excited me to self-activity. I sincerely hope it will do the same for you.

Joseph Sutton
San Francisco, 1991

Achievement

Having once decided to achieve a certain task, achieve it at all costs of tedium and distaste. The gain in self-confidence of having accomplished a tiresome labor is immense. —Arnold Bennett

Happiness lies not in the mere possession of money; it lies in the joy of achievement, in the thrill of creative effort. —Franklin Delano Roosevelt

My mother drew a distinction between achievement and success. She said that achievement is the knowledge that you have studied and worked hard and done the best that is in you. Success is being praised by others, and that's nice, too, but not as important or satisfying. Always aim for achievement and forget about success. —Helen Hayes

So to conduct one's life as to realize oneself—this seems to me the highest attainment possible to a human being. —Henrik Ibsen

1

To achieve great things we must live as though we were never going to die.

—Marquis de Vauvenargues

One never notices what has been done; one can only see what remains to be done.   —Marie Curie

We never do anything well till we cease to think about the manner of doing it.   —William Hazlitt

Anybody can be Pope; the proof of this is that I have become one.   —Pope John XXIII

> Let us then be up and doing
> With a heart for every fate
> Still achieving, still pursuing
> Learn to labor and to wait.
> —Henry Wadsworth Longfellow

Action

You can't expect to hit the jackpot if you don't put a few nickels in the machine.   —Flip Wilson

All the beautiful sentiments in the world weigh less than a single lovely action.   —James Russell Lowell

Action may not always bring happiness; but there is no happiness without action. —Benjamin Disraeli

To reach the port of heaven we must sail, sometimes with the wind and sometimes against it—but we must sail, not drift or lie at anchor.
—Oliver Wendell Holmes, Sr.

Get action. Do things; be sane, don't fritter away your time . . . take a place wherever you are and be somebody; get action. —Theodore Roosevelt

The man who tried his best and failed is superior to the man who never tried. —Bud Wilkinson

The great end of life is not knowledge, but action.
—T.H. Huxley

Make up your mind to act decidedly and take the consequences. No good is ever done in this world by hesitation. —T.H. Huxley

Dare to be wise; begin! He who postpones the hour of living rightly is like the rustic who waits for the river to run out before he crosses. —Horace

We should be taught not to wait for inspiration to start a thing. Action always generates inspiration. Inspiration seldom generates action. —Frank Tibolt

The ideal day never comes. Today is ideal for him who makes it so.   —HORATIO DRESSER

The end of man is action, and not a thought, though it were the noblest.   —THOMAS CARLYLE

Doubt, of whatever kind, can be ended by Action alone.   —THOMAS CARLYLE

Nothing will ever be attempted if all possible objections must be first overcome.   —SAMUEL JOHNSON

We are made for action, and for right action—for thought and for true thought. Let us live while we live; let us be alive and doing; let us act on what we have.
                    —JOHN HENRY CARDINAL NEWMAN

An ounce of practice is worth a pound of preaching.
                    —OLD PROVERB

Count that day lost whose low descending sun
Views from thy hand no worthy action done.
                    —ANONYMOUS

Hope in every sphere of life is a privilege that attaches to action. No action, no hope.   —PETER LEVI

Strong reasons make strong actions.
                    —SHAKESPEARE

A person who believes in something, who acts on what seems really important, always finds the energy to accomplish the task. —Dennis T. Jaffee
—Cynthia D. Scott

I do not believe in a fate that falls on men however they act; but I do believe in a fate that falls on them unless they act. —G.K. Chesterton

Even if you're on the right track, you'll get run over if you just sit there. —Will Rogers

We lose much by fearing to attempt.
—J.N. Moffitt

Go ahead with your life, your plans, your preparation, as fully as you can. Don't waste time by stopping before the interruptions have started.
—Richard L. Evans

Trust only movement. Life happens at the level of events not of words. Trust movement.
—Alfred Adler

Of all sad words of tongue or pen,
The saddest are these: It might have been.
—John Greenleaf Whittier

And if not now, when?
—The Talmud

One must fight for a life of action, not reaction.
—RITA MAE BROWN

Action is the proper Fruit of Knowledge.
—THOMAS FULLER

To live is not merely to breathe, it is an act; it is to make use of our organs, senses, faculties, of all those parts of ourselves which give us the feeling of existence. —JEAN JACQUES ROUSSEAU

Aging

Age is strictly a case of mind over matter. If you don't mind, it doesn't matter. —JACK BENNY

Grow old along with me!
The best is yet to be.
—ROBERT BROWNING

If I'd known I was going to live so long, I'd have taken better care of myself. —LEON ELDRED

Growing old is no more than a bad habit which a busy man has no time to form. —ANDRE MAUROIS

As you get older and the light at the end of the tunnel becomes more obvious, you realize that you need good health to carry you the distance. You realize that it would be hell on earth to be sick, imprisoned in an old body that wasn't quite ready to die yet.

—BOB RYAN

Age to me means nothing. I can't get old; I'm working. I was old when I was twenty-one and out of work. As long as you're working, you stay young.

—GEORGE BURNS

The aging process has you firmly in its grasp if you never get the urge to throw a snowball.

—DOUG LARSON

Old age isn't so bad when you consider the alternative.

—MAURICE CHAVALIER

To me old age is always fifteen years older than I am.

—BERNARD BARUCH

I shall grow old, but never lose life's zest,
Because the road's last turn will be the best.

—HENRY VAN DYKE

Anyone can get old. All you have to do is live long enough.

—GROUCHO MARX

Cato learned Greek at eighty; Sophocles
Wrote his grand Oedipus, and Simonides
Bore off the price for verse from his compeers,
When each had numbered more than fourscore years.
—HENRY WADSWORTH LONGFELLOW

There is no such thing as "on the way out." As long
as you are still doing something interesting and good,
you're in business because you're still breathing.
—LOUIS ARMSTRONG

Today I have completed 64 Springtimes and I am now
in much better health, much stronger, much more active, than I ever was in my youth. It is quite wrong to
think of old age as a downward slope. One climbs
higher and higher with the advancing years, with surprising strides.   —GEORGE SAND (AMANDINE DUPIN)

As long as you are useful, you'll never be old.
—LEO BUSCAGLIA

I have discovered the secret formula for a carefree Old
Age: ICR-FI—"If You Can't Recall It, Forget It."
—GOODMAN ACE

Whatever a man's age, he can reduce it several years
by putting a bright-colored flower in his buttonhole.
—MARK TWAIN

If you live long enough, the venerability factor creeps in: you get accused of things you never did and praised for virtues you never had. —I.F. STONE

There's many a good tune played on an old fiddle.
—OLD PROVERB

Age is not a question of years but of constitution and temperament. —CHAUNCEY DEPEW

At fifty a man's real life begins. He has acquired upon which to achieve; received from which to give; learned from which to teach; cleared upon which to build.
—E.W. BOK

Old age, to the unlearned, is winter; to the learned, it is harvest time. —JUDAH LEIB LAZEROV

Tranquility is the *summum bonum* of old age.
—THOMAS JEFFERSON

How old would you be if you didn't know how old you was? —LEROY (SATCHEL) PAIGE

If you're going to get old you might as well get as old as you can get. —WALLACE STEGNER

The riders in a race do not stop short when they reach the goal. There is a little finishing canter before coming to a standstill. There is time to hear the kind voice of friends and to say to one's self: "The work is done."
—OLIVER WENDELL HOLMES, JR.

Old age is no such uncomfortable thing, if one gives oneself up to it with a good grace.
—HORACE WALPOLE

Every age can be enchanting, provided you live within it.
—BRIGITTE BARDOT

It's not how old you are, it's how hard you work at it.
—JONAH BARRINGTON

Men are like wine—some turn to vinegar, but the best improve with age.
—POPE JOHN XXIII

Old age takes away from us what we have inherited and gives us what we have earned.
—GERALD BRENAN

As I approach my middle 70s, they don't—or I don't—seem old at all. I am disconcerted to realize how old that seemed to me when I was in my middle 60s. I remember attending friends' 75th birthdays, astonished that they could still get around.
—PAGE SMITH

Alone/Solitude

All men's miseries derive from not being able to sit quiet in a room alone. —BLAISE PASCAL

They are never alone that are accompanied with noble thoughts. —PHILIP SIDNEY

By all means use sometimes to be alone. Salute thyself; see what thy soul doth wear. —GEORGE HERBERT

The capacity to be alone becomes linked with self-discovery and self-realization; with becoming aware of one's deepest needs, feelings, and impulses.
—ANTHONY STORR

I am never less alone than when alone.
—SCIPIO AFRICANUS

In solitude, where we are LEAST alone.
—LORD BYRON

Solitude is as needful to the imagination as society is wholesome for the character.
—JAMES RUSSELL LOWELL

I never found the companion that was so companionable as solitude.   —HENRY DAVID THOREAU

If you make friends with yourself you will never be alone.   —MAXWELL MALTZ

It is better to be alone than in ill company.
                                —GEORGE PETTIE

The happiest of all lives is a busy solitude.
                                —VOLTAIRE

You do not need to leave your room. Remain sitting at your table and listen. Do not even listen, simply wait. Do not even wait, be quite still and solitary. The world will freely offer itself to you to be unmasked, it has no choice, it will roll in ecstasy at your feet.
                                —FRANZ KAFKA

Solitude: A good place to visit, but a poor place to stay.
                        —JOSH BILLINGS (H.W. SHAW)

It is easy in the world to live after the world's opinions; it is easy in solitude to live after our own; but the Great Man is he who in the midst of the crowd keeps with perfect sweetness the independence of solitude.
                        —RALPH WALDO EMERSON

The best thinking has been done in solitude. The worst
has been done in turmoil.   —Thomas Edison

Talent is best nurtured in solitude.

—Goethe

Solitude, though it may be silent as light, is, like light,
the mightiest of agencies; for solitude is essential to
man.   —Thomas De Quincey

Solitude makes us love ourselves.

—A.B. Alcott

In solitude alone can be known true freedom.

—Michel de Montaigne

The thoughtful soul to solitude retires.

—Omar Khayyam

Get away from the crowd when you can. Keep yourself to yourself, if only for a few hours daily.

—Arthur Brisbane

Anger/Temper

When you are angry say nothing and do nothing until you have recited the alphabet.
—Athenodorus Cananites

When angry, count four; when very angry, swear.
—Mark Twain

He who restrains his anger overcomes his greatest enemy.
—Latin Proverb

We are all crazy when we are angry.
—Philemon

If you are patient in one moment of anger, you will escape a hundred days of sorrow.
—Chinese Proverb

You need some positive ways to express and process your anger or it will destroy you. A therapist who uses body release work would be excellent. Writing a "hate letter" and then burning it would help. So would sitting in front of a mirror and telling the person in question all the things you're angry about. Running or playing tennis are also good outlets, as are screaming in the car or beating the bed or kicking pillows.
—Louise L. Hay

How much more grievous are the consequences of anger than the causes of it.　　—MARCUS AURELIUS

When you are offended at any man's fault, turn to yourself and study your own failings. Then you will forget your anger.　　—EPICTETUS

Peace of mind is better than giving them "a piece of your mind."　　—J.P. McEVOY

Anger is only one letter short of danger.
　　—ANONYMOUS

No man can think clearly when his fists are clenched.
　　—GEORGE JEAN NATHAN

Anger is never without a reason, but seldom with a good one.　　—BENJAMIN FRANKLIN

Anger blows out the lamp of the mind.
　　—ROBERT INGERSOLL

People who fly into a rage always make a bad landing.
　　—WILL ROGERS

The best cure for anger is delay.
　　—SENECA

I don't do anything that's bad for me. I don't like to be made nervous or angry. Any time you get upset it tears down your nervous system.   —MAE WEST

Be not hasty in thy spirit to be angry: for anger resteth in the bosom of fools.   —BIBLE, ECCLESIASTES

Anger and temper shorten our years.
                                —JEWISH PROVERB

He who restrains his temper will have all his sins forgiven.   —JEWISH PROVERB

A perverse temper and fretful disposition will make any state of life whatsoever unhappy.   —CICERO

Never do anything when you are in a temper, for you will do everything wrong.   —BALTASAR GRACIÁN

All healthy things are sweet-tempered.
                                —RALPH WALDO EMERSON

Good temper, like a sunny day, sheds a brightness over everything; it is the sweetener of toil and the soother of disquietude.   —WASHINGTON IRVING

Good temper is an estate for life.
                                —WILLIAM HAZLITT

Apathy/Indifference

What the world needs is some "do-give-a-damn" pills.
—WILLIAM C. MENNINGER

The worst sin towards our fellow creatures is not to hate them, but to be indifferent to them: that's the essence of inhumanity.   —GEORGE BERNARD SHAW

The opposite of life is not death, it's indifference.
—ELIE WIESEL

Mourn not the dead . . .
But rather mourn the apathetic throng—
The cowed and meek
Who see the world's great anguish and its wrong,
And dare not speak.
—RALPH CHAPLIN

Where apathy is the master, all men are slaves.
—ANONYMOUS

Neutral men are the devil's allies.
—EDWIN HUBBEL CHAPIN

Aspirations

Far away there in the sunshine are my highest aspirations. I may not reach them, but I can look up and see their beauty, believe in them, and try to follow where they lead. —LOUISA MAY ALCOTT

Our aspirations are our possibilities.
—ROBERT BROWNING

A noble aim, faithfully kept, is as a noble deed.
—WILLIAM WORDSWORTH

> Climb High
> Climb Far
> Your goal the sky
> Your aim the star.
> —INSCRIPTION ON HOPKINS MEMORIAL STEPS,
> WILLIAMS COLLEGE, WILLIAMSTOWN, MA.

Before you begin a thing, remind yourself that difficulties and delays quite impossible to foresee are ahead. If you could see them clearly, naturally you could do a great deal to get rid of them but you can't. You can only see one thing clearly and that is your goal. Form a mental vision of that and cling to it through thick and thin. —KATHLEEN NORRIS

There are two things to aim at in life: first, to get what you want; and, after that, to enjoy it. Only the wisest of mankind can achieve the second.

—LOGAN PEARSALL SMITH

Aim at the sun, and you may not reach it; but your arrow will fly higher than if aimed at an object on a level with yourself. —JOEL HAWES

Before you can score, you must first have a goal.

—GREEK PROVERB

Goals are potent.

—WILL McCOY

The person who makes a success of living is the one who sees his goal steadily and aims for it unswervingly.

—CECIL B. DEMILLE

Know what you want to do, hold the thought firmly, and do every day what should be done, and every sunset will see you that much nearer the goal.

—ELBERT HUBBARD

To remain healthy, man must have some goal, some purpose in life that he can respect and be proud to work for. —HANS SELYE

Arriving at one goal is the starting point to another.

—JOHN DEWEY

The world turns aside to let any man pass who knows whither he is going.   —DAVID STARR JORDAN

First say to yourself what you would be; and then do what you have to do.   —EPICTETUS

The great thing in this world is not so much where we are, but in what direction we are moving.
                    —OLIVER WENDELL HOLMES, SR.

We need objectives. We need focus and direction. Most of all, we need the sense of accomplishment that comes from achieving what we set out to do . . . it's important to make plans, even if we decide to change them, so that at least for the moment we know where we're going and we can have a sense of progress.
                    —LEON TEC, M.D.

Life means to have something definite to do—a mission to fulfill—and in the measure in which we avoid setting our life to something, we make it empty. Human life, by its very nature, has to be dedicated to something.   —JOSE ORTEGA Y GASSET

Nothing is particularly hard if you divide it into small jobs.   —HENRY FORD

It is a matter first of beginning—and then following through.   —RICHARD L. EVANS

You have to work to make it work.

—ALAN BLUM

Let us be resolute in attaining our ends, and mild in our method of attainment. —AQUAVIVA

Ideals are like the stars. You will not succeed in touching them with your hands; but, like the seafaring man, you choose them as your guides, and, following them, you will reach your destiny. —CARL SCHURZ

Don't part with your ideals. They are anchors in a storm. —ARNOLD H. GLASOW

No wind favors him who has no destined port.

—MICHEL DE MONTAIGNE

Why not go out on a limb? Isn't that where the fruit is?

—FRANK SCULLY

He who has a why to live can bear almost any how.

—FRIEDRICH NEITZSCHE

A man without a plan for the day is lost before he starts. —LEWIS K. BENDELE

Make no little plans; they have no magic to stir men's blood . . . .Make big plans, aim high in hope and work.

—DANIEL H. BURNHAM

A man needs a purpose for real health.
—Sherwood Anderson

The secret of success is constancy to purpose.
—Benjamin Disraeli

Have a purpose in life, and having it throw into your work such strength of mind and muscle as God has given you.   —Thomas Carlyle

The great and glorious masterpiece of man is how to live with a purpose.   —Michel de Montaigne

This is our purpose: to make as meaningful as possible this life that has been bestowed upon us; to live in such a way that we may be proud of ourselves; to act in such a way that some part of us lives on.
—Oswald Spengler

Attitude/Disposition

The greater part of our happiness or misery depends on our dispositions and not on our circumstances.
—Martha Washington

Happiness is an endowment and not an acquisition. It depends more upon temperament and disposition than environment. —JOHN J. INGALLS

When fate hands us a lemon, let's try to make a lemonade. —DALE CARNEGIE

A man is generally as happy as he makes up his mind to be. —ABRAHAM LINCOLN

> Lay aside life-harming heaviness
> And entertain a cheerful disposition.
> —SHAKESPEARE

Sourness spoils men as well as milk.
—B.C. FORBES

Disease is a kind of consolidation of a mental attitude, and it is only necessary to treat the mind of a patient and the disease will disappear. —DR. EDWARD BACH

Man being made a reasonable, and so a thinking creature, there is nothing more worthy of his being than the right direction and employment of his thoughts; since upon this depends both his usefulness to the public, and his own present and future benefit in all respects. —WILLIAM PENN

I must say in all honesty that I do not see any technique [cure] that is outstandingly better than any other. So much depends on the individual's temperament and willingness to heal and be healed.   —STEPHEN LEVINE

It all depends on how we look at things, and not on how they are in themselves.   —CARL JUNG

Everything can be taken from a man but one thing: the last of the human freedoms—to choose one's attitude in any given set of circumstances, to choose one's own way.   —VIKTOR E. FRANKL

One thing I have learned is that attitudes should not be underestimated in any assessment of the healing equation.   —NORMAN COUSINS

If thou art pained by any external thing, it is not this thing that disturbs thee, but thy own judgment about it. And it is in thy power to wipe out this judgment now.   —MARCUS AURELIUS

The fountain of content must spring up in the mind; and he who has so little knowledge of human nature as to see his happiness by changing anything but his own disposition, will waste his life in fruitless efforts, and multiply the griefs which he proposes to remove.   —SAMUEL JOHNSON

The longer we dwell on our misfortune, the greater is their power to harm us. —VOLTAIRE

The world improves people according to the dispositions they bring into it. —RENIER GIUSTINA MICHAEL

Positive attitudes—optimism, high self-esteem, an outgoing nature, joyousness, and the ability to cope with stress—may be the most important bases for continued good health. —HELEN HAYES

Why do some people always see beautiful skies and grass and lovely flowers and incredible human beings, while others are hard-pressed to find anything or any place that is beautiful? —LEO BUSCAGLIA

Beauty, madam, pleases the eyes only; sweetness of disposition charms the soul. —VOLTAIRE

What life means to us is determined not so much by what life brings to us as by the attitude we bring to life; not so much by what happens to us as by our reaction to what happens. —LEWIS L. DUNNINGTON

Beauty

Beauty, and the most perfect health is the most perfect beauty.
—WILLIAM SHENSTONE

That which is striking and beautiful is not always good, but that which is good is always beautiful.
—NINON DE LENCLOS

I don't think of all the misery, but of the beauty that still remains . . . .Go outside, to the fields, enjoy nature and the sunshine, go out and try to recapture happiness in yourself and in God. Think of all the beauty that's still left in and around you and be happy.
—ANNE FRANK

Cheerfulness and content are great beautifiers, and are famous preservers of youthful looks.
—CHARLES DICKENS

Exuberance is Beauty.
—WILLIAM BLAKE

Zest is the secret of all beauty. There is no beauty that is attractive without zest.   —CHRISTIAN DIOR

Even the ugliest human exteriors may contain the most beautiful viscera.   —JOHN B.S. HALDANE

Beauty is how you feel inside and it reflects in your eyes. It is not something physical.   —SOPHIA LOREN

A thing of beauty is a joy forever: Its loveliness increases; it will never pass into nothingness.
    —JOHN KEATS

The longer I live the more beautiful life becomes.
    —FRANK LLOYD WRIGHT

What is beautiful is good, and who is good will soon be beautiful.   —SAPPHO

Beauty is its own excuse for being.
    —RALPH WALDO EMERSON

Though we travel the world over to find the beautiful, we must carry it with us or we find it not.
    —RALPH WALDO EMERSON

There is nothing more beautiful than cheerfulness in an old face.   —JEAN PAUL RICHTER

Beauty is the only thing that time cannot harm. Philosophies fall away like sand, and creeds follow one another like the withered leaves of Autumn; but what is beautiful is a joy for all seasons and a possession for all eternity. —OSCAR WILDE

Perfect health, like perfect beauty, is a rare thing . . . .
—PETER MERE LATHAM

Health and wealth create beauty.
—H.G. BOHN

Digestion exists for health, and health exists for life, and life exists for the love of music and beautiful things. —G.K. CHESTERTON

Body

The body never lies.
—MARTHA GRAHAM

Your body knows perfectly well what's good for it.
—SHAKTI GAWAIN

The body is a cell state in which every cell is a citizen.
—RUDOLF VIRCHOW

The body is the baggage you must carry through life.
The more excess baggage, the shorter the trip.
—Arnold H. Glasow

But for our body one whole realm of God's glory—
all that we receive through the senses—would go un-
praised. For the beasts can't appreciate it and the
angels are, I suppose, pure intelligence.
—C.S. Lewis

The best cure for hypochondria is to forget about your
body and get interested in someone else's.
—Goodman Ace

The human body is the best picture of the human soul.
—Ludwig Wittgenstein

The body mirrors the soul and the mind, and is much
more accessible than either.   —Dr. George Sheehan

A man ought to handle his body, like the sail of a ship,
and neither lower and reduce it much when no cloud
is in sight, nor be slack and careless in managing it
when he comes to suspect something is wrong.
—Plutarch

Health and good estate of body are above all good.
—Bible, Ecclesiasticus

The human body is the magazine of inventions, the patent office, where are the models from which every hint is taken. All the tools and engines on earth are only extensions of its limbs and senses.

—Ralph Waldo Emerson

The remarkable life force possessed by the body, the body's ability to heal its own wounds and mend its broken bones, indeed, the very wisdom shown by the body.

—Richard E. DeRoeck

If any thing is sacred, the human body is sacred,
And the glory and sweet of a man is the token
   of manhood untainted,
And in man or woman a clean, strong, firm-fibred
   body is more beautiful than the most beautiful face.

—Walt Whitman

Body and Soul

Safeguard the health both of body and soul.

—Cleobulus

Half the spiritual difficulties that men and women suffer arise from a morbid state of health.

—Henry Ward Beecher

A bodily disease which we look upon as whole and entire within itself, may, after all, be but a symptom of some ailment in the spiritual part.

—Nathaniel Hawthorne

A healthy body is a guest-chamber of the soul; a sick body, its prison.   —Francis Bacon

Coddle the body and you harm the soul.

—Polish Proverb

Those who see any difference between soul and body have neither.   —Oscar Wilde

The physical is the substratum of the spiritual; and this fact ought to give to the food we eat, and the air we breathe, a transcendent significance.

—William Tyndale

There are more pernicious diseases of the soul than of the body.   —Cicero

The soul is a mere spectator of the movements of its body.   —Charles Bonnet

The body is the workhouse of the soul.

—H.G. Bohn

There is nothing the body suffers that the soul may not profit by. —GEORGE MEREDITH

Busy

The really idle man gets nowhere. The perpetually busy man does not get much further.
—HENEAGE OGILVIE

None are so busy as the fool and knave.
—JOHN DRYDEN

Ever busy, ever bare.
—JAMES KELLY

A man too busy to take care of his health is like a mechanic too busy to take care of his tools.
—SPANISH PROVERB

It's not enough to be busy . . . the question is: What are we busy about? —HENRY DAVID THOREAU

I'm as busy as ever, and that's the secret when you get older. Don't stop working, always keep busy and active, that's important. —LOUIS J. LEFKOWITZ

The busy man has few idle visitors; to the boiling pot the flies come not.　　　　　—BENJAMIN FRANKLIN

The busier we are, the more acutely we feel that we live, the more conscious we are of life.

—IMMANUEL KANT

Those who have most to do, and are willing to work, will find the most time.　　　　　—SAMUEL SMILES

The greatest happiness comes from the greatest activity.　　　　　—C.D. BOVEE

We are so busy, we have so much on our minds, that we don't feel anything any more. We are also impatient, so we don't notice what we really feel.

—ERICH FROMM

Character/Discipline

To keep your character intact you cannot stoop to filthy acts. It makes it easier to stoop the next time.
—KATHARINE HEPBURN

When wealth is lost, nothing is lost;
When health is lost, something is lost;
When character is lost, all is lost!
—GERMAN PROVERB

This above all; to thine own self be true,
And it must follow, as the night the day,
Thou canst not be false to any man.
—SHAKESPEARE

The measure of a man's real character is what he would do if he knew he would never be found out.
—THOMAS MACAULAY

The late Babe Didrikson Zaharias once disqualified herself from a tournament for having hit the wrong ball out of the rough. "But nobody would have known," a friend told her. "I would've known," Babe replied.
—DAVE ANDERSON

I care not what others think of what I do, but I care very much about what I think of what I do: That is character! —THEODORE ROOSEVELT

I am different from Washington. I have a higher, grander standard of principle. Washington could not lie. I *can* lie, but I won't. —MARK TWAIN

It is when a man ceases to do the things he has to do, and does the things he likes to do, that the character is revealed. It is when the repressions of society and business are gone and when the goads of money and fame and ambition are lifted, and man's spirit wanders where it listeth, that we see the inner man, his real self.
—LIN YUTANG

It matters not what you are thought to be, but what you are. —PUBLILIUS SYRUS

Character is like a tree and reputation like its shadow. The shadow is what we think of it; the tree is the real thing. —ABRAHAM LINCOLN

To be persuasive, we must be believable.
To be believable, we must be credible.
To be credible, we must be truthful.
—EDWARD R. MURROW

Be true to yourself though the heavens fall.
—EUGENE O'NEILL

It is not the brains that matter most, but that which
guides them—the character, the heart, generous qual-
ities, progressive ideas.   —FEODOR DOSTOEVSKY

Man's character is his fate.
—HERACLITUS

Don't compromise yourself. You are all you've got.
—JANIS JOPLIN

You cannot dream yourself into a character; you must
hammer and forge yourself one.   —JAMES A. FROUDE

Sow a thought, reap an act;
Sow an act, reap a habit;
Sow a habit, reap a character;
Sow a character, reap a destiny.
—ANONYMOUS

Character is simply a habit continued.
—PLUTARCH

Good habits are not made on birthdays, nor Christian character at the new year. The workshop of character is everyday life. The uneventful and commonplace hour is where the battle is lost or won.
—MALTBIE D. BABCOCK

Character is nurtured midst the tempests of the world.
—GOETHE

Character is higher than intellect. Thinking is the function. Living is the functionary.
—RALPH WALDO EMERSON

For a man to be a man and not a robot, he is going to have to work at creating his character. He is going to have to work at being true to himself. He is going to have to work at knowing himself and thinking for himself. He is going to have to work at learning, at growing.   —JOSEPH RAYMOND

The true index of a man's character is the health of his wife.   —CYRIL CONNOLLY

You've got to learn to survive a defeat. That's when you develop character.   —RICHARD M. NIXON

Do not consider painful what is good for you.
—EURIPEDES

No horse gets anywhere until he is harnessed. No steam or gas ever drives anything until it is confined. No Niagara is ever turned into light and power until it is tunneled. No life ever grows great until it is focused, dedicated, disciplined. —HARRY EMERSON FOSDICK

We have no greater or lesser conquest than over ourselves. —LEONARDO DA VINCI

There is only one reason why men become addicted to drugs; they are weak men. Only strong men are cured, and they cure themselves. —MARTIN H. FISCHER

What you want to be eventually, that you must be every day; and by and by the quality of your deeds will get down into your soul. —FRANK CRAVE

Some people regard discipline as a chore. For me, it is a kind of order that sets me free to fly. —JULIE ANDREWS

Discipline is making sure that you do what is good for you. —BILL SAKS

Power over oneself is better than a thousand years of power over others. —FUDAIL IBN AYAD

Cheerfulness/Joy

Cheerfulness keeps up a kind of daylight in the mind, and fills it with a steady and perpetual serenity.

—JOSEPH ADDISON

I felt an earnest and humble desire, and shall do till I die, to increase the stock of harmless cheerfulness.

—CHARLES DICKENS

Let us be of good cheer, remembering that the misfortunes hardest to bear are those which never come.

—AMY LOWELL

The best way to cheer yourself up is to try to cheer somebody else up.

—MARK TWAIN

Cheerfulness is the very flower of health.

—JAPANESE PROVERB

Every heart that has beat strong and cheerfully has left a hopeful impulse behind it in the world, and bettered the tradition of mankind.

—ROBERT LOUIS STEVENSON

Continual cheerfulness is a sign of wisdom.

—Irish Proverb

> What of the outer drear,
> As long as there's inner light;
> As long as the sun of cheer
> Shine ardently bright?
>
> —John Kendrick Bangs

Health and cheerfulness mutually beget each other.

—Joseph Addison

Cheerfulness, sir, is the principal ingredient in the composition of health. —Arthur Murphy

Health is the condition of wisdom, and the sign of cheerfulness. —Ralph Waldo Emerson

A merry heart maketh a cheerful countenance.

—Bible, Proverbs

The joyfulness of a man prolongeth his days.

—Bible, Ecclesiasticus

Real joy comes not from ease or riches or from the praise of men, but from doing something worthwhile.

—Wilfred T. Grenfell

The only joy in the world is to begin.
                              —CESARE PAVESE

A joy that's shared is a joy made double.
                              —JOHN RAY

Joy is not in things; it is in us.
                              —RICHARD WAGNER

Those who bring sunshine to the lives of others cannot keep it from themselves.   —ANONYMOUS

Joy comes in our lives when we have something to do, something to love, and something to hope for.
                              —JOSEPH ADDISON

One joy scatters a hundred griefs.
                              —OLD PROVERB

Joy . . . is found only in the good things of the soul.
                              —PHILO

Let joy be your compass heading.
                              —ANONYMOUS

Healing is simply attempting to do more of those things that bring joy into your life.
                              —O. CARL SIMONTON

Join the whole creation of animate things in a deep, heartfelt joy that you are alive, that you see the sun, that you are in this glorious earth which nature has made so beautiful, and which is yours to conquer and enjoy. —WILLIAM OSLER

Live merrily as thou canst, for by honest mirth we cure many passions of the mind. —ROBERT BURTON

Conscience

My wealth is health and perfect ease;
My conscience clear my chief defense.
—EDWARD DYER

Look to your health; and if you have it, praise God, and value it next to a good conscience, for health is the second blessing that we mortals are capable of; a blessing that money cannot buy. —IZAAK WALTON

There is no pillow so soft as a clear conscience.
—FRENCH PROVERB

Reason deceives us often; conscience never.
—JEAN JACQUES ROUSSEAU

The only tyrant I accept in this world is the "still small voice" within me.　　　　　　　—GANDHI

When conscience discovers nothing wrong, what is there to be uneasy about, what is there to fear?
　　　　　　　—CONFUCIUS

In the midst of all the doubts which we have discussed for four thousand years in four thousand ways, the safest course is to do nothing against one's conscience. With this secret, we can enjoy life and have no fear from death.　　　　　　　—VOLTAIRE

Conscience is a thousand witnesses.
　　　　　　　—RICHARD TAVERNER

A clear conscience needeth no excuse, nor feareth any accusation.　　　　　　　—JOHN LYLY

A good conscience is a continual feast.
　　　　　　　—ROBERT BURTON

Conscience is the perfect interpreter of life.
　　　　　　　—KARL BARTH

Never do anything against conscience even if the state demands it.　　　　　　　—ALBERT EINSTEIN

The only religion is conscience in action.
—HENRY DEMAREST LLOYD

Conscience is God's presence in man.
—EMANUEL SWEDENBORG

Conscience: the inner voice which warns us that someone may be looking. —H.L. MENCKEN

Be a master of your will and a slave of your conscience. —JEWISH PROVERB

If you don't manage your own life, how are you going
to sleep at night? —TOM SEAVER

The first and indispensable requisite of happiness is a
clear conscience, unsullied by the reproach or remem-
brance of an unworthy action. —EDWARD GIBBON

Cowardice asks the question, "Is it safe?" Expediency
asks the question, "Is it politic?" Vanity asks the question, "Is it popular?" But conscience asks the question,
"Is it right?" And there comes a time when one must
take a position that is neither safe, nor politic, nor
popular, but he must take it because his conscience
tells him it is right. —MARTIN LUTHER KING, JR.

All a man can betray is his conscience.
—JOSEPH CONRAD

I feel within me
A peace above all earthly dignities,
A still and quiet conscience.

—SHAKESPEARE

A good eater must be a good man; for a good eater
must have a good digestion, and a good digestion depends upon a good conscience.

—BENJAMIN DISRAELI

There is no witness so terrible, no accuser so potent,
as the conscience that dwells in every man's breast.

—POLYBIUS

The laws of conscience, though we ascribe them to nature, actually come from custom.

—MICHEL DE MONTAIGNE

Friends, books, a cheerful heart, and a conscience clear
Are the most choice companions we have here.

—WILLIAM MATHER

My conscience is my crown,
  Contented thoughts my rest;
My heart is happy in itself;
  My bliss is in my breast.

—ROBERT SOUTHWELL

Contentment

With only plain rice to eat, with only water to drink, and with only an arm for a pillow, I am still content.
—Confucius

Fortify yourself with contentment, for this is an impregnable fortress.
—Epictetus

The contented mind is the only riches, the only quietness, the only happiness.
—George Pettie

Content is more than kingdom.
—English Proverb

When we cannot find contentment in ourselves it is useless to seek it elsewhere.
—La Rochefoucauld

My crown is in my heart, not on my head;
Not deck'd with diamonds and Indian stones,
Nor to be seen: my crown is called content;
A crown it is that seldom kings enjoy.
—Shakespeare

Enjoy your own life without comparing it with that of another.
—Marquis de Condorcet

From labor, health; from health, contentment springs.
—JAMES BEATTIE

Who lives content with little possesses everything.
—NICOLAS BOILEAU

Riches are not from an abundance of worldly goods, but from a contented mind.   —MOHAMMED

In order to be content, men must have the possibility of developing their intellectual and artistic powers to whatever extent accords with their personal characteristics and abilities.   —ALBERT EINSTEIN

Reflect on your present blessings, of which every man has many, not on your past misfortunes, of which all men have some.   —CHARLES DICKENS

We can learn to use our minds rather than be used by them. To do this means learning to practice contentment.   —JOAN BORYSENKO

The world is full of people looking for spectacular happiness while they snub contentment.
—DOUG LARSON

Contentment is natural wealth, luxury is artificial poverty.   —SOCRATES

True contentment is a real, even an active virtue—not only affirmative but creative. It is the power of getting out of any situation all there is in it.

　　　　　　　　　　　　　　　　—G.K. CHESTERTON

If you are but content, you have enough to live upon with comfort.　　　　　　　　　　　—PLAUTUS

True contentment depends not upon what we have; a tub was large enough for Diogenes, but a world was too little for Alexander.　　　　　—C.C. COLTON

Contentment consisteth not in adding more fuel, but in taking away some fire; not in multiplying wealth, but in subtracting men's desires.　　—THOMAS FULLER

Content has a kindly influence on the soul of man, in respect of every being to whom he stands related. It extinguishes all murmuring, repining, and ingratitude toward that Being who has alloted us our part to act in the world. It destroys all inordinate ambition; gives sweetness to the conversation, and serenity to all the thoughts; and if it does not bring riches, it does the same thing by banishing the desire of them.

　　　　　　　　　　　　　　　　—JOSEPH ADDISON

If we fasten our attention on what we have, rather than on what we lack, a very little wealth is sufficient.

　　　　　　　　　　　　　　　　—F. JOHNSON

He is truly happy who has all that he wishes to have, and wishes to have nothing which he ought not to wish.　　　　　　　　　　—St. Augustine

My first goal was spiritual satisfaction. If I was able to have that then that would breed contentment. If I had contentment it wouldn't matter what I had because I wouldn't want anything.　　　—Dr. Richard Diamond

> I have mental joys and mental health,
> Mental friends and mental wealth,
> I've a wife that I love and that loves me;
> I've all but riches bodily.
> 　　　　　　　　　—William Blake

The greatest wealth is contentment with a little.
　　　　　　　　　　　　　　　—John Ray

Countryside/Nature

> Before green apples blush
> 　Before green nuts embrown,
> Why, one day in the country
> 　Is worth a month in town.
> 　　　　　　　　　—Christina Rossetti

Seldom shall we see in cities, courts, and rich families, where men live plentifully, and eat and drink freely, that perfect health and athletic soundness and vigor of constitution which are commonly seen in the country, where nature is the cook, and necessity the caterer, and where they have no other doctor but the sun and fresh air.　　　　　　　　　　　—ROBERT SOUTH

I go to Nature to be soothed and healed, and to have my senses put in tune once more.
　　　　　　　　　　　　　　—JOHN BURROUGHS

I have loved the feel of the grass under my feet, and the sound of the running streams by my side. The hum of the wind in the treetops has always been good music to me, and the face of the fields has often comforted me more than the faces of men.　　—JOHN BURROUGHS

　On the trail marked with pollen may I walk
　With grasshoppers about my feet may I walk
　With dew about my feet may I walk
　With beauty may I walk.
　　　　　　　　　　—AMERICAN INDIAN POEM

It becomes necessary occasionally, simply to throw open the hatches and ventilate one's psyche, or whatever you choose to call it. This means an excursion to some place where the sky is not simply what you see at the end of the street.　　—LOUIS J. HALLE

In nature you can hear the beat of your own heart and the sound of your own footsteps. Take yourself there as often as you can—to the sea, to the mountains, to the forests and meadows. In nature you can learn that you are part of a grand and beautiful scheme and that you are as valid a part of life's masterpiece as is everything that you see around you.   —MARILYN DIAMOND

We must go out and re-ally ourselves to Nature every day. We must take root, send out some little fibre at least, even every winter day.
—HENRY DAVID THOREAU

You must converse much with the field and woods, if you would imbibe such health into your mind and spirit as you covet for your body.
—HENRY DAVID THOREAU

Climb the mountains and get their tidings. Nature's peace will flow into you as sunshine flows into trees. The winds will blow their own freshness into you, and the storms their energy, while cares will drop away from you like the leaves of Autumn.   —JOHN MUIR

There is something infinitely healing in the repeated refrains of nature—the assurance that dawn comes after night, and spring after winter.
—RACHEL CARSON

The country for a wounded heart.
—ENGLISH PROVERB

Oh, the content, the quiet, the plenty of the Russian open country! Oh, the deep peace and well being.
—IVAN TURGENEV

> The little cares that fretted me,
>   I lost them yesterday
> Among the fields above the sea,
>   Among the winds at play;
> Among the lowing of the herds,
>   The rustling of the trees,
> Among the singing of the birds,
>   The humming of the bees.
> —ANONYMOUS

The divinest things—religion, love, truth, beauty, justice—seem to lose their meaning and value when we sink into lassitude and indifference . . . .It is a signal that we should quit meditation and books, and go out into the open air, into the presence of nature, into the company of flocks and children, where we may drink new health and vigor from the clear and full flowing fountains of life, afar from the arid wastes of theory and speculation; where we may learn again that it is not by intellectual questionings, but by believing, hoping, loving, and doing that man finds joy and peace.
—JOHN LANCASTER SPALDING

The outdoors is what you have to pass through to get from your apartment into a taxicab [in New York City].
—FRAN LEBOWITZ

The love of Nature . . . helps us greatly to keep ourselves free from those mean and petty cares which interfere so much with calm and peace of mind.
—JOHN LUBBOCK

The country life is to be preferred, for there we see the works of God . . . .The country is both the philosopher's garden and library, in which he reads and contemplates the power, wisdom, and goodness of God.
—WILLIAM PENN

. . . the sanctuary and special delight of kings, where, laying aside their cares, they withdraw to refresh themselves with a little hunting; there, away from the turmoils inherent in a court, they breathe freedom.
—RICHARD FITZNIGEL

I want to go fishing! somewhere on a stream
I want to give way to the longing to a dream
Away from the tumult of motor and mill
I want to be care-free; I want to be still!
I'm weary of doing things; weary of words
I want to be one with the blossoms and birds.
—EDGAR A. GUEST

Cure

The best cure for worry, depression, melancholy, brooding, is to go deliberately forth and try to lift with one's sympathy the gloom of somebody else.
—ARNOLD BENNETT

To cure bad health, think nothing unclean.
—PUBLILIUS SYRUS

A good laugh and a long sleep are the best cures in the doctor's book.   —IRISH PROVERB

Who pays the physician does the cure.
—GEORGE HERBERT

The art of medicine consists of amusing the patient while nature cures the disease.   —VOLTAIRE

It is part of the cure to wish to be cured.
—SENECA

Here is a mental treatment guaranteed to cure every ill that flesh is heir to: sit for half an hour every night and mentally forgive everyone against whom you have any ill will or antipathy.   —CHARLES FILLMORE

The wise, for cure, on exercise depend.

—JOHN DRYDEN

Learning to let go of negative emotions is key.

—DR. BERNIE SIEGEL

I believe that all genuine healing addresses the problem of unblocking negativities in one way or another.

—SUN BEAR

For me, the healing process is made up of unconditional love, forgiveness, and letting go of fear. It is that simple.　　　—GERALD JAMPOLSKY

Nature, time and patience are the three great physicians.　　　—CHINESE PROVERB

Keep your head cool, your feet warm, and you'll make the best doctor poor.　　　—DR. HERMAN BOERHAVE

Purge the blood of its poisons and it becomes a flowing fountain of youth.　　　—ALEXIS CARRELL, M.D.

The cure for grief is motion.

—ELBERT HUBBARD

There is no cure for birth and death, save to enjoy the interval.　　　—GEORGE SANTAYANA

Many dis-eases come from polluting our bodies. We all need to go back to more natural ways of living. Nutritionally, this includes eating more fruits, vegetables, and whole grains. It also encompasses deep breathing, getting adequate exercise, and loving ourselves.

—Louise L. Hay

It is certain that the personality without conflict is immune from illness. —Dr. Edward Bach

The presence of the doctor is the first part of the cure.

—French Proverb

Death

It's not that I'm afraid to die, I just don't want to be there when it happens. —WOODY ALLEN

I think of death only with tranquility, as an end. I refuse to let death hamper life. Death must enter life only to define it. —JEAN PAUL SARTRE

Thus that which is the most awful of evils, death, is nothing to us, since when we exist there is no death, and when there is death we do not exist. —EPICURUS

Perhaps the best cure for the fear of death is to reflect that life has a beginning as well as an end. There was a time when we were not; this gives us no concern—why then should it trouble us that a time will come when we shall cease to be? —WILLIAM HAZLITT

I adore life but I don't fear death. I just prefer to die as late as possible.   —GEORGES SIMENON

He that fears death, lives not.
                              —GEORGE HERBERT

It is true that I am carrying out various methods of treatment recommended by doctors and dentists in the hope of dying in the remote future in perfect health.
                              —GEORGE SANTAYANA

I want to be healthy when I die.
                              —JOSEPH RAYMOND

Two out of every three deaths are premature; they are related to loafer's heart, smoker's lung and drinker's liver.   —DR. THOMAS J. BASSLER

Death . . . is no more than passing from one room into another. But there's a difference for me, you know. Because in that other room I shall be able to see.
                              —HELEN KELLER

If you do not know how to die, don't worry. Nature herself will teach you in the proper time; she will discharge that work for you; don't trouble yourself.
                              —MICHEL DE MONTAIGNE

Everybody has got to die, but I have always believed an exception would be made in my case. Now what?
—WILLIAM SAROYAN

When a man dies, he does not just die of the disease he has, he dies of his entire life! —CHARLES PÉGUY

You learn something the day you die. You learn how to die. —KATHERINE ANNE PORTER

I don't believe in dying. It's been done. I'm working on a new exit. Besides, I can't die now—I'm booked.
—GEORGE BURNS

Shrinking away from death is something unhealthy and abnormal which robs the second half of life of its purpose. —CARL JUNG

To die will be an awfully big adventure.
—JAMES M. BARRIE

Do not fear death so much, but rather the inadequate life. —BERTOLT BRECHT

Death is not the greatest loss in life. The greatest loss is what dies inside us while we live.
—NORMAN COUSINS

Death is not a failure. Not choosing to take on the challenge of life is.   —DR. BERNIE SIEGEL

If we can learn to view death from a different perspective, to reintroduce it into our lives so that it comes not as a dreaded stranger but as an expected companion to our life, then we can also learn to live our lives with meaning—with full appreciation of our finiteness, of the limits on our time here.

—ELISABETH KÜBLER-ROSS

For those who seek to understand it, death is a highly creative force. The highest spiritual values of life can originate from the thought and study of death.

—ELISABETH KÜBLER-ROSS

If you can live your life and die as natural a death as possible, I think this is what we should work for. This is the only reason to have any good health at all, so we don't have to retire before we die.

—BERNARD JENSEN

The goal in life is to die young—as late as possible.

—ASHLEY MONTAGU

You ought to be afraid to die until you've contributed something great back to humanity.

—OLIVER WENDELL HOLMES, SR.

Of all escape mechanisms, death is the most efficient.
—H.L. MENCKEN

Die, my dear doctor—that's the last thing I shall do.
—LORD PALMERSTON

A good life has a peaceful death.
—FRENCH PROVERB

It is a poor thing for anyone to fear that which is inevitable.
—TERTULLIAN

To die well is to die willingly.
—SENECA

It matters not how a man dies, but how he lives. The act of dying is of no importance, it lasts so short a time.
—SAMUEL JOHNSON

The more you think of dying the better you will live.
—ITALIAN PROVERB

A long illness between life and death makes death a comfort to those who die and to those who remain.
—JEAN DE LA BRUYÈRE

Digestion

If you want to clear your system out, sit on a piece of cheese and swallow a mouse.   —JOHNNY CARSON

Digestion is the great secret of life.
—SYDNEY SMITH

His sleep was aery light, from pure digestion bred.
—JOHN MILTON

To eat is human; to digest, divine.
—CHARLES TOWNSEND COPELAND

I have finally come to the conclusion that a good reliable set of bowels is worth more to a man than any quantity of brains.   —JOSH BILLINGS (H.W. SHAW)

The fate of a nation has often depended upon the good or bad digestion of a prime minister.   —VOLTAIRE

Now good digestion wait on appetite,
And health on both!
—SHAKESPEARE

Disability

Cripple is beautiful!
— DAVID AVERBUCK, A PARAPLEGIC

Each of us must find out for himself that his handicaps, his failures, and shortcomings must be conquered or else he must perish . . . .My weakness—my handless-ness—my sense of inferiority has turned out to be my greatest strength. It's not what you have lost, but what you have left that counts . . . .I was able to meet the challenge of utter disaster and master it. For me, this was and is the all important fact—that the human soul, beaten down, overwhelmed, faced by complete failure and ruin, can still rise up against unbearable odds and triumph.   — HAROLD RUSSELL

Be willing to have it so. Acceptance of what has hap-pened is the first step to overcoming the consequences of any misfortune.   — WILLIAM JAMES

The first thing you have to do after suffering a stroke is to tell yourself you won't give up, that you don't want to die, or be cared for like a baby the rest of your life . . . .Now I'm healthy and have only a slight limp and some trouble remembering the names of people and places. But I get better every year, and I'm still working.   — PATRICIA NEAL

One day a classmate asked him what had caused him to become so badly crippled. "Infantile paralysis," said the young man on crutches. "With a misfortune like that," said his friend, "how can you face the world so confidently and happily?" "Because," replied the polio victim, "the disease never reached my heart."
—EDWARD GIBBON

You are not crippled at all unless your mind is in a splint.   —FRANK SCULLY

If I could give a message to the physically disabled, it would be this: Overcome self-pity by reaching out to others like you and giving them courage and support. Lift others and you lift yourself. Meet each challenge that your handicap brings with faith; don't give up, no matter what. Be as independent and self-reliant as possible. Educate yourself. And lastly, discover your talents and use them!   —VIRL OSMOND

Disease/Sickness

The beginning of health is to know the disease.
—MIGUEL DE CERVANTES

Disease is an experience of so-called mortal mind. It is fear made manifest on the body.

—MARY BAKER EDDY

Every disease is a doctor.

—IRISH PROVERB

What we call disease is nothing more than the body's own effort to cleanse itself of toxins.

—DR. JOHN H. TILDEN

The causes of all diseases are to be found in the blood.

—JEWISH PROVERB

Life is in the blood, health is in the blood. When the blood does not properly circulate, cells die or become abnormal. This leads to disease.

—DR. NATHANIEL S. WIRT

Nature, in the production of disease, is uniform and consistent, so much so, that for the same disease in different persons the symptoms are for the most part the same; and the selfsame phenomena that you would observe in the sickness of a Socrates you would observe in the sickness of a simpleton.

—THOMAS SYDENHAM

There is a common argument that is both false and fatal. "So-and-so," one hears, "has been cured by such-and-such a treatment, and I have his disease; *ergo*, I must try his remedy." How many people die by reasoning thus! What they overlook is that the diseases which afflict us are different as the features of our faces.   —VOLTAIRE

We do not see disease as occurring the same way in every person. Disease is as individual as individuals are.   —DR. TRIVEDI, AYURVEDIC TEACHER

Sometimes it is more important to know what kind of patient has a disease than what kind of disease the patient has.   —WILLIAM OSLER

The most costly disease in America is not cancer or coronaries. The most costly disease is boredom—costly for both individual and society.
                                            —NORMAN COUSINS

It requires great and long-continued abuse of the body to reduce its functions sufficiently to produce the state of impaired health known as disease.
                                            —HARVEY DIAMOND

Disease is an energy crisis of the body.
                                            —MARILYN DIAMOND

The diseases of the present have little in common with the diseases of the past save that we die of them.

—AGNES REPPLIER

Seriousness is a fatal disease.

—PAUL ZAMARIAN

Serious illness doesn't bother me for long because I am too inhospitable a host. —ALBERT SCHWEITZER

The more serious the illness, the more important it is for you to fight back, mobilizing all your resources— spiritual, emotional, intellectual, physical.

—NORMAN COUSINS

You have got to fight against illness as if you were Mike Tyson in the ring, pummeling and pouncing on it fast and hard. —JOSEPH RAYMOND

Much illness is unhappiness sailing under a physiologic flag. —RUDOLF VIRCHOW

The process of illness is a result of the body's attempts to heal itself. —GEORGE GOODHEART

Sickness is a belief, which must be annihilated by the divine Mind. —MARY BAKER EDDY

Illness is telling us what we need to stop doing. If we look at illness that way, then it has great value. It might be telling us that we need to modify our work habits, to rest, or to question what we are doing . . . .It forces us to reach out for help, bringing more love to us.

—O. CARL SIMONTON

Rather than thinking of illness as disaster, we can think of it as a powerful and useful message. If we are suffering, it is a message that there is something to be looked at within our consciousness, something to be recognized, acknowledged, and healed.   —SHAKTI GAWAIN

To hate and to fear is to be psychologically ill. It is, in fact, the consuming illness of our time.

—H.A. OVERSTREET

As some sharpness gives a better relish to sweet meats, so some sense of sickness makes us taste the benefit of health.   —BRILLIANA HARLEY

How sickness enlarges the dimension of a man's self to himself! He is his own exclusive object. He has nothing to think of but how to get well.

—CHARLES LAMB

I'd prefer to die than to be sick. The only thing for me is health; all the rest you can hustle.

—HARRY DE WILDT

Health is not valued till sickness comes.
—THOMAS FULLER

Be not sick too late, nor well too soon.
—BENJAMIN FRANKLIN

Sickness arrives on horseback and departs on foot.
—WALLOON PROVERB

Most of the time we think we're sick, it's all in the mind.
—THOMAS WOLFE

The feeling of health is acquired only by sickness.
—G.C. LICHTENBERG

Do not be sick. The sick man is more than half a rascal. He may only be sick because he hasn't the courage to clean house. Many sick people are bullies—they use sickness as a club to beat others.
—SHERWOOD ANDERSON

We can no longer be useful when not well.
—SAMUEL JOHNSON

True, God sends us colds—but according to our clothes.
—JEWISH PROVERB

Those who neglect to keep their feet dry are suicides.
—JOHN ABERNATHY

He who sits with his back to a draft sits with his face
to a coffin. —SPANISH PROVERB

And he that will his health deny,
Down among the dead men let him lie.
—JOHN DYER

Three things drain a man's health: worry, travel, and
sin. —THE TALMUD

Despise no new accident in your body, but ask opinion of it. —FRANCIS BACON

Some people are so sensitive that they feel snubbed if
an epidemic overlooks them.
—FRANCIS MCKINNEY HUBBARD

When a man loses his health, then he first begins to
take good care of it. —JOSH BILLINGS (H.W. SHAW)

Doctor and Patient

The doctor of the future will give no medicine but will interest his patients in the care of the human frame, in diet, and in the cause and prevention of disease.
— THOMAS EDISON

Medicine is not only a science, but also the art of letting our own individuality interact with the individuality of the patient. — ALBERT SCHWEITZER

[It is best if doctors] care more for the individual patient than for the special features of the disease.
— WILLIAM OSLER

I believe that the common denominator of all healing methods is unconditional love—a love that respects the uniqueness of each individual client and empowers the client to take responsibility for his or her own well-being. — JACK SCHWARZ

Love received and love given comprise the best form of therapy. — GORDON W. ALLPORT

It is this intangible thing, love, love in many forms, which enters into every therapeutic relationship. It is an element of which the physician may be the carrier, the vessel. And it is an element which binds and heals, which comforts and restores, which works what we have to call—for now—miracles.

—KARL A. MENNINGER

The most important focus of therapy is that of teaching people how to feel and express love. And this, I have found, depends on my ability to love them and show them they are lovable.   —DR. BERNIE SIEGEL

While the patient wants the best and most modern treatment available, he is also badly in need of the old-fashioned friend that a doctor has always personified.

—DR. GUNNAR GUNDERSON

The role of the physician and other health care workers is to empower patients—to help them to take charge of their own lives.   —CLIVE WOOD

The attitude of the healer is almost as important as the attitude of the person being healed.

—O. CARL SIMONTON

Most doctors seldom consider how a patient's attitude towards life shapes that life's quantity and quality.

—DR. BERNIE SIEGEL

Doctors must learn to give patients the option to participate in recovery from *any* type of disease.

—Dr. Bernie Siegel

It is no exaggeration to say that many people get better simply because they like the doctor.

—George Goodheart

The patient's hopes are the physician's best ally.

—Norman Cousins

I don't believe that one person heals another. I believe that what we do is invite the other person into a healing relationship. We heal together.

—Dr. Rachel Naomi Remen

The patient must combat the disease along with the physician.

—Hippocrates

Keep up the spirits of your patient with the music of the viol and the psaltery, or by forging letters telling of the death of his enemies, or (if he be a cleric) by informing him that he has been made a bishop.

—Henri de Mondeville

What I call a good patient is one who, having found a good physician, sticks to him till he dies.

—Oliver Wendell Holmes, Sr.

Patients worry over the beginning of an illness; doctors worry over its end.   —CHINESE PROVERB

In treating a patient, let your first thought be to strengthen his natural vitality.   —RHAZES

Doctors/Physicians

Physicians, of all men, are most happy; whatever good success soever they have, the world proclaimeth, and what faults they commit, the earth covereth.
—FRANCIS QUARLES

If the doctor cures, the sun sees it; if he kills, the earth hides it.   —ANONYMOUS

Physician: One upon whom we set our hopes when ill, and our dogs when well.   —AMBROSE BIERCE

The more doctors, the more sickness.
—PORTUGUESE PROVERB

I am dying with the help of too many physicians.
—ALEXANDER THE GREAT

I wondher why ye can always read a doctor's bill an' ye niver can read his purscription.

—Finley Peter Dunne

Never go to a doctor whose office plants have died.

—Erma Bombeck

When a doctor looks me square in the face and kant see no money in me, then i am happy.

—Josh Billings (H.W. Shaw)

> When at last we are sure
> You've been properly pilled
> Then a few paper forms
> Must be properly filled
> So that you and your heirs
> May be properly billed.
>
> —Dr. Seuss (Theodore Geisel)

Fresh air keeps the doctor poor.

—Danish Proverb

Where there is sunshine the doctor starves.

—Flemish Proverb

We had for three weeks past a warm visit from the sun (my almighty physician) and I find myself almost reestablished.

—Thomas Jefferson

Optimistic lies have such immense therapeutic value that a doctor who cannot tell them convincingly has mistaken his profession.   —GEORGE BERNARD SHAW

The great secret of doctors, known only to their wives, but still hidden from the public, is that most things get better by themselves; most things, in fact, are better in the morning.   —DR. LEWIS THOMAS

Our apothecary's shop is our garden full of potherbs, and our doctor is a clove of garlic.   —ANONYMOUS

Kinship is healing; we are physicians to each other.
—OLIVER SACKS

Joy and Temperance and Repose
Slam the door on the doctor's nose.
—HENRY WADSWORTH LONGFELLOW

The first was called Doctor Diet, the second Doctor Quiet, the third Doctor Merryman.
—WILLIAM BULLEIN

If doctors fail you, let these three be your doctors: a cheerful mind, rest, and moderate diet.
—ANONYMOUS

Temperance and labor are the two true physicians of man. Labor sharpens his appetite and temperance prevents him abusing it.   —JEAN JACQUES ROUSSEAU

No man is more worthy of esteem than a physician who, having studied nature from his youth, knows the properties of the human body, the diseases which assail it, and the remedies which will benefit it, who exercises his art with caution, and who gives equal attention to the rich and the poor.   —VOLTAIRE

Doctors pour drugs of which they know little, to cure diseases of which they know less, into human beings of whom they know nothing.   —VOLTAIRE

Strive to preserve your health; and in this you will the better succeed in proportion as you keep clear of the physicians, for their drugs are a kind of alchemy concerning which there are no fewer books than there are medicines.   —LEONARDO DA VINCI

He's the best physician that knows the worthlessness of the most medicines.   —BENJAMIN FRANKLIN

Some people think that doctors and nurses can put scrambled eggs back into the shell.
     —DOROTHY CANFIELD FISHER

A doctor gets no pleasure out of the health of his friends. —MICHEL DE MONTAIGNE

They that be whole need not a physician.
—BIBLE, MATTHEW

Perfect obedience to the laws of health would abolish the medical profession. —O.B. FROTHINGHAM

Every doctor has something of the shaman, a talent for infecting people with hope and positive attitudes that heals as it uplifts. —DR. STEVEN LOCKE
—DOUGLAS COLLIGAN

It is our duty as physicians . . . to hold aloft the light, and the name of that light is hope.
—KARL MENNINGER

Future doctors will clearly understand the mechanism of disease. They will know what goes wrong and be able to prevent, even reverse, the process.
—LISA M. KRIEGER

It takes a wise doctor to know when not to prescribe.
—BALTASAR GRACIÁN

Doing

Better do it than wish it done.

—SCOTTISH PROVERB

From saying to doing is a long step.

—ITALIAN PROVERB

Let us then be up and doing, with a heart for any fate.

—HENRY WADSWORTH LONGFELLOW

If you're able to and want to, then do—for the life to come may be an awful bust.

—WILLIAM CARLOS WILLIAMS

Just do it!

—BUMPER STICKER, 1980S

Most of the things worth doing in the world had been declared impossible before they were done.

—LOUIS BRANDEIS

The doer is better than the critic, and the man who strives stands far above the man who stands aloof.

—THEODORE ROOSEVELT

To do anything in this world worth doing, we must not stand back shivering and thinking of the cold and danger, but jump in, and scramble through as well as we can. —SYDNEY SMITH

Do it now. It is not safe to leave a generous feeling to the cooling influences of the world.
—THOMAS GUTHRIE

Things won are done; joy's soul lies in the doing.
—SHAKESPEARE

One can only do by doing.
—FRENCH PROVERB

Our grand business undoubtedly is, not to *see* what lies dimly at a distance, but to *do* what lies clearly at hand.
—THOMAS CARLYLE

When you must, you can.
—JEWISH PROVERB

When one decides that something becomes top priority, then one goes out and does it.
—ANONYMOUS

Doing is what matters.
—ROBERT COLES

It is not what we do, but how we do it.

—STEPHEN LEVINE

So find out what you want to be, and do, and take off your coat, and make a dust in the world.

—CHARLES READE

It is the greatest of all mistakes to do nothing because you can do only a little. Do what you can.

—SYDNEY SMITH

I came to understand that it was all right to do things for people as long as I did it for the sake of doing it . . . the value being more in the act than in the result.

—JOANNA FIELD

The world is moving so fast these days that the man who says it can't be done is generally interrupted by someone doing it.

—ELBERT HUBBARD

Doubt

If you doubt you can accomplish something, then you can't accomplish it. You have to have confidence in your ability, and then be tough enough to follow through.

—ROSALYNN CARTER

Our doubts are traitors,
And make us lose the good we oft might win,
By fearing to attempt.
—SHAKESPEARE

Doubt indulged soon becomes doubt realized.
—FRANCIS RIDLEY HAVERGAL

He that doubteth is damned.
—BIBLE, ROMANS

The only limit to our realization of tomorrow will be our doubts of today.   —FRANKLIN D. ROOSEVELT

Doubt whom you will, but never doubt yourself.
—C.D. BOVEE

Happy are those who have no doubt of themselves.
—GUSTAVE FLAUBERT

Doubt is the key to knowledge.
—PERSIAN PROVERB

I respect faith, but doubt is what gets you an education.   —WILSON MIZNER

He that knows nothing, doubts nothing.
—GEORGE HERBERT

Faith and doubt both are needed—not as antagonists but working side by side—to take us around the unknown curve. —Lillian Smith

Modest doubt is call'd
The beacon of the wise.
—Shakespeare

Thought only starts with doubt.
—Roger Martin Du Gard

Just think of the tragedy of teaching children not to doubt. —Clarence Darrow

With a little doubt, there is a small awakening.
With great doubt, there is a great awakening.
With no doubt, there is no awakening.
—Zen Saying

We know accurately only when we know little; with knowledge doubt enters. —Goethe

Men become civilized, not in proportion to their willingness to believe, but in proportion to their readiness to doubt. —H.L. Mencken

If a man will begin with certainties, he will end in doubts; but if he will be content to begin with doubts, he will end in certainties. —Francis Bacon

Doubt is an incentive to truth and patient inquiry leadeth the way. —HOSEA BALLON

Materialists and madmen never have doubts.
—G.K. CHESTERTON

The trouble with the world is that the stupid are cock-sure and the intelligent are full of doubt.
—BERTRAND RUSSELL

In all affairs it's a healthy thing now and then to hang a question mark on the things you have long taken for granted. —BERTRAND RUSSELL

When in doubt, punt.
—AMERICAN SAYING

Dreams

The best way to make your dreams come true is to wake up. —PAUL VALÉRY

Hold fast to dreams for if dreams die,
Life is a broken-winged bird that cannot fly.
—LANGSTON HUGHES

If you don't have a dream, then how can your dream come true?   —Dr. Richard Diamond

The poor man is not he who is without a cent, but he who is without a dream.   —Harry Kemp

To accomplish great things, we must dream as well as act.   —Anatole France

> Hold fast your dreams!
> Within your heart
> Keep one still, secret spot
> Where dreams may go,
> And, sheltered so,
> May thrive and grow
> Where doubt and fear are not.
> O keep a place apart,
> Within your heart,
> For little dreams to go!
>   —Louise Driscoll

Dreams are the touchstones of our characters.
                    —Henry David Thoreau

Go confidently in the direction of your dreams! Live the life you've imagined. As you simplify your life, the laws of the universe will be simpler, solitude will not be solitude, poverty will not be poverty, nor weakness weakness.   —Henry David Thoreau

If you have built castles in the air, your work need not be lost; that is where they should be. Now put foundations under them. —HENRY DAVID THOREAU

There are no rules of architecture for a castle in the clouds. —G.K. CHESTERTON

Reach high, for stars lie hidden in your soul. Dream deep, for every dream precedes the goal. —PAMELA VAULL STARR

Don't part with your illusions. When they are gone, you may still exist, but you have ceased to live. —MARK TWAIN

We must select the illusion which appeals to our temperament, and embrace it with passion if we want to be happy. —CYRIL CONNOLLY

Drinking

O God, that men should put an enemy
in their mouths to steal away their brains!
—SHAKESPEARE

It's all right to drink like a fish—if you drink what a
fish drinks. —MARY PETTIBONE POOLE

I don't drink. I don't like it. It makes me feel good.
—OSCAR LEVANT

One reason I don't drink is that I want to know when
I am having a good time. —NANCY ASTOR

We drink one another's healths and spoil our own.
—JEROME K. JEROME

Temperate men drink the most, because they drink the
longest. —C.C. COLTON

Bacchus hath drowned more men than Neptune.
—THOMAS FULLER

Long quaffing maketh a short life.
—JOHN LYLY

Drink not the third glass—which thou can'st not tame
when once it is within thee. —GEORGE HERBERT

What's drinking?
A mere pause from thinking.
—LORD BYRON

Drink injures a man externally, internally, and eternally.   —ANONYMOUS

Drinking a little too much is drinking a great deal too much.   —GERMAN PROVERB

Drunkenness is the ruin of reason. It is premature old age. It is temporary death.   —ST. BASIL

Drinking makes such fools of people, and people are such fools to begin with, that it's compounding a felony.   —ROBERT BENCHLEY

One swallow doesn't make a summer but too many swallows make a fall.   —G.D. PRENTICE

A drunkard is like a whiskey bottle, all neck and belly and no head.   —AUSTIN O'MALLEY

Abstaining is favorable both to the head and the pocket.   —HORACE GREELEY

Drinking makes holes in your pocket.
                                                    —MEXICAN PROVERB

No, thank you, I was born intoxicated.
          —GEORGE WILLIAM RUSSELL, REFUSING A DRINK
          OFFERED HIM.

One martini is all right, two is too many, three is not enough. —JAMES THURBER

The best cure for drunkenness is, when sober, to look at a drunken man. —CHINESE PROVERB

Drunkenness is simply voluntary insanity. —SENECA

But I'm not so think as you drunk I am. —JOHN COLLINGS SQUIRE

Take that liquor away; I never touch strong drink. I like it too well to fool with it. —STONEWALL JACKSON

Odd, people spend their lives filling themselves with booze, then when it gets them, they act like they never expected it. —BOB RYAN

The man who is master of himself drinks gravely and wisely. —CONFUCIUS

If the husband drinks, half the house is afire; if the wife drinks, the whole house. —RUSSIAN PROVERB

The smaller the drink, the clearer the head, and the cooler the blood. —WILLIAM PENN

Eating/Diet

One meal a day—a man is a yogi.
Two meals a day—he is a *bhogi* [enjoyer].
Three meals a day—he is a *rogi* [glutton].
Four meals a day—carry him to the cremation grounds.
—INDIAN SAYING

Short supper; long life.

—SERBIAN PROVERB

Reverse the typical American meal pattern and instead eat like a king for breakfast, a prince for lunch and a pauper for supper.   —JANE E. BRODY

Stop short of your appetite; eat less than you are able.
—OVID

Feed by measure, and defy the physician.
—JOHN HEYWOOD

One should eat to live; not live to eat.

—CICERO

Some people have a foolish way of not minding, or pretending not to mind, what they eat. For my part, I mind my belly very studiously and very carefully, for I look upon it that he who does not mind his belly will hardly mind anything else.   —SAMUEL JOHNSON

Tell me what you eat, and I will tell you what you are.

—ANTHELME BRILLAT-SAVARIN

If you wish to grow thinner, diminish your dinner,
    And take to light claret instead of pale ale;
Look down with an utter contempt upon butter,
    And never touch bread till it's toasted—or stale.

—H.S. LEIGH

Slow eating and good mastication are essential for good health. Never eat in a hurry. Never eat when not really hungry. Always eat in a relaxed atmosphere— and *enjoy* what you eat.   —PAAVO AIROLA

Part of the secret of success in life is to eat what you like and let the food fight it out inside.

—MARK TWAIN

If it grows, eat it. If it doesn't grow, don't eat it.

—LOUISE L. HAY

The more natural the food you eat, the more radiant health you will enjoy.   —PATRICIA BRAGG

Eat a variety of foods; maintain a desirable weight; avoid too much fat; eat foods with adequate starch and fiber; avoid too much sugar and sodium; and, if you drink alcohol, drink in moderation.
> —SURGEON GENERAL OF THE UNITED STATES, 1989.

Everything you eat affects you profoundly.
> —CHINESE PROVERB

If you are building a thirty-story building and you use worm-eaten wood for the frame, inferior structural supports, and other fourth-rate, low-grade materials, what kind of finished product do you think you will wind up with? No need to answer. So if you're building a human body and the material that will become your blood, bones, skin, organs—indeed, *every* cell of your body—is inferior and of poor quality, what kind of body do you think you will wind up with? No need to answer.   —HARVEY DIAMOND

To keep from gaining weight, don't eat late.
> —JEANETTE SUTTON

Healthful eating can load the odds in your favor.
> —JIM WOOD

Nature does her best to teach us. The more we over-eat, the harder she makes it for us to get close to the table.   —EARL WILSON

Who eats of but one dish never needs a physician.
                                    —ITALIAN PROVERB

Man is what he eats.
                                    —L.A. FEUERBACH

Leave thy drugs in the chemist's pot if thou can't heal the patient with food.   —HIPPOCRATES

Food is man's only truly reliable medicine and foods do cure, just the same as wrong foods and drinks may kill us.   —BERNARD JENSEN

Diet cures more than doctors.
                                    —A.B. CHEALES

Food is an important part of a balanced diet.
                                    —FRAN LEBOWITZ

The allegory of Adam and Eve eating of the tree of evil, and entailing upon their posterity the wrath of God and the loss of everlasting life, admits of no other explanation than the disease and crime that have flowed from unnatural diet.   —PERCY BYSSHE SHELLEY

Sermons on diet ought to be preached in the churches at least once a week.   —G.C. LICHTENBERG

Now learn what and how great benefits a temperate diet will bring. In the first place you enjoy good health.
          —HORACE

Diet away your stress, tension and anxiety; a new commonsense plan for the control of low blood sugar related disorders, including overeating and obesity, migraine headaches, alcoholism, mental disturbances, hypoglycemia and hyperactivity.   —J. DANIEL PALM

Restricting the fat in the diet allows more oxygen into our tissue cells, so we will feel more energetic. You have to rid your system of the excess fat and aerate it to feel your most alive, alert, and energetic.
          —NATHAN PRITIKIN

If we just ate the diet of prehistoric man—peanuts in the shell, apple cores, cactus fruit and an occasional ant—and with the advances of modern medicine, proper exercise and the pampered lifestyle we have, there's no reason we couldn't make it to a hundred years old.   —VAUGHN BRYANT, JR., ANTHROPOLOGIST

Probably nothing in the world arouses more false hopes than the first four hours of a diet.
          —DAN BENNETT

Internal cleanliness depends on diet, and we should choose everything that is clean and wholesome and as fresh as possible, chiefly natural fruits, vegetables and nuts.   —DR. EDWARD BACH

Whatsoever was the father of a disease, an ill diet was the mother.   —GEORGE HERBERT

A little with quiet is the only diet.
                                                    —OLD PROVERB

Ecology

Hurt not the earth, neither the sea, nor the trees.
                                        —BIBLE, REVELATIONS

The first law of ecology is that everything is related to everything else.   —BARRY COMMONER

Conservation means development as much as it does protection. I recognize the right and duty of this generation to develop and use the natural resources of our land; but I do not recognize the right to waste them, or to rob, by wasteful use, the generations that come after us.   —THEODORE ROOSEVELT

To live healthily and successfully on the land, we must also live with it. We must be part not only of the human community, but of the whole community. . . . Ours is not only "one world"...it is also "one earth."
—Joseph Wood Krutch

The earth is our mother. We must take care of her.
—Anonymous

We are beginning to remember and understand that living in harmony with mother earth is more important than almost anything else. And, in the process of learning how to live in harmony on the earth, people will understand more about their own psyches.
—Lynn Andrews

The white man must treat the beasts of this land as his brothers. For whatever happens to the beasts soon happens to man. All things are connected.
—Chief Seattle

By seeing that we are truly one with all things, we see that in supporting the killing of others or the destruction of the natural world, we are inviting that destruction upon ourselves. With this realization we begin the true healing, which means coming into resonance with the creator's one law: *You shall be in good relationship with each other and with all things in the Great Circle of Life.*
—Brooke Medicine Eagle

The frog does not drink up the pond in which he lives.
—BUDDHIST PROVERB

What's one more candy wrapper on a city street? . . .
Just add one more soft-drink can . . . one more bit of
orange peel . . . one more matchbook . . . one more
cigar butt . . . you can build a mountain of garbage in
no time.
—THE AMERICAN MUSEUM OF NATURAL HISTORY,
NEW YORK

Let everyone sweep in front of his or her own door,
and the whole world will be clean.   —GOETHE

Everyone is looking for a technological bandaid for the
automobile air pollution problem. The answer is walking. It's so logical, it's absurd.   —BRIAN KETCHAM

Each time one of us walks someplace instead of driv-
ing, that much less poison has been injected into the
air we all breathe. (Actually the benefits are multiple.
One less car means that the rest of the traffic will move
that much more quickly and burn less fuel.)
—JOHN P. WILEY, JR.

In a sense, earth is our collective body. The way we
treat her mirrors the way we treat our bodies.
—SHAKTI GAWAIN

You look down at this planet and it's all one living system.   —RUSSELL SCHWEICKART, ASTRONAUT

As cruel a weapon as the cave man's club, the chemical barrage has been hurled against the fabric of life.
                                        —RACHEL CARSON

I became an ecologist long before I heard the word.
                                    —FRANCISCO MENDES

Effort

I will spit on my hands and take better hold.
                                    —JOHN HEYWOOD

If at first you don't succeed,
Try, try, try again.
                                —WILLIAM E. HICKSON

There is no failure except in no longer trying.
                                    —ELBERT HUBBARD

If we want to keep living with ourselves, we must keep on trying, trying, trying.   —ROBERT J. WHITE, M.D.

Keep trying. It's only from the valley that the mountain seems high.   —ANONYMOUS

It is common sense to take a method and try it. If it fails, admit it frankly and try another. But above all, try something.   —FRANKLIN D. ROOSEVELT

You may be disappointed if you fail, but you are doomed if you don't try.   —BEVERLY SILLS

Little and often make much.

—ANONYMOUS

There are no useless efforts. Sisyphus was developing his muscles.   —ROGER CALLOIS

Whatever thy hand findeth to do, do it with all thy might.   —BIBLE, ECCLESIASTES

I always remember an epitaph which is in the cemetery at Tombstone, Arizona. It says: "Here lies Jack Williams. He done his damndest." I think that is the greatest epitaph a man can have—when he gives everything that is in him to do the job he has before him. That is all you can ask of him and that is what I have tried to do.   —HARRY S. TRUMAN

Whatever is worth doing at all is worth doing well.

—EARL OF CHESTERFIELD

Don't waste your time striving for perfection; instead, strive for excellence—doing your best.

—LAURENCE OLIVIER

As the old man walked the beach at dawn, he noticed a young man ahead of him picking up starfish and flinging them into the sea. Finally catching up with the youth, he asked him why he was doing this. The answer was that the stranded starfish would die if left until the morning sun. "But the beach goes on for miles and there are millions of starfish," countered the other. "How can your effort make any difference?" The young man looked at the starfish in his hand and then threw it to safety in the waves. "It makes a difference to that one," he said.

—MINNESOTA LITERACY COUNCIL

I am only me, but still I am one
I cannot do everything, but still
   I can do something,
And because I cannot do everything,
I will not refuse to do the something
   that I can do.

—TOASTMASTERS TREASURE CHEST

Give what you have. To someone it may be better than you dare to think.

—HENRY WADSWORTH LONGFELLOW

When we do the best that we can, we never know what miracle is wrought in our life, or in the life of another.

—HELEN KELLER

Doing anything well means not merely getting the job done. We are probably very capable of quantity work when we want to be. But it's the quality work—the kind we can step back from and admire today and for years to come—that is what really counts.

—AMY E. DEAN

It is for us to make the effort. The result is always in God's hands.

—GANDHI

Continuous effort—not strength or intelligence—is the key to unlocking our potential.

—LIANE CORDES

One is happy as the result of one's own efforts.

—GEORGE SAND (AMANDINE DUPIN)

One is always seeking the touchstone that will dissolve one's deficiencies as a person and a craftsman. And one is always bumping up against the fact there is none except hard work, concentration and continued application.

—PAUL GALLICO

The hard part of making good is that you have to do it every day.   —ANONYMOUS

Emotions/Feelings

What's a human interest story without pain and anger, love and joy? Emotions are the very stuff of life.
                              —JOAN BORYSENKO

Negative emotions will not harm you if you express them appropriately and then let them go. Bottling them up is far worse.   —JOAN BORYSENKO

Strong emotion has a way of finding routes of expression. If not recognized and dealt with for what it is, it may manifest as pain or illness.
                              —MARTIN L. ROSSMAN, M.D.

Cherish your own emotions and never undervalue them.   —ROBERT HENRI

The emotions may be endless. The more we express them, the more we may have to express them.
                              —E.M. FORSTER

Never apologize for showing feeling. When you do so, you apologize for truth.   —BENJAMIN DISRAELI

Do not violence to yourself; respect in yourself the oscillations of feeling: they are your life and your nature; a wiser than you made them.   —HENRI F. AMIEL

When you give vent to your feelings, anger leaves you.
—JEWISH PROVERB

> I was angry with my friend:
> I told my wrath, my wrath did end.
> I was angry with my foe:
> I told it not, my wrath did grow.
> —WILLIAM BLAKE

If a man can cry, then he has feelings. Indians cry all the time. We get together and sing songs, and we cry in these songs. But this society is very machine-like, and so we begin to act like machines and then we become machines.   —WILFRED PELLETIER

Only one absolute certainty is possible to man, namely, that at any given moment the feeling which he has exists.   —T.H. HUXLEY

Love God and trust your feelings. Be loyal to them. Don't betray them.   —ROBERT C. POLLOCK

You cannot control the external circumstances of your life, but you can control your reactions to them.

—JOAN BORYSENKO

Learning to be aware of feelings, how they arise and how to use them creatively so they guide us to happiness, is an essential lifetime skill. —JOAN BORYSENKO

Surprising as it seems, when we let go of our feelings and start to be totally honest with ourselves, we find greater and deeper and lovelier emotions to express.

—SEFRA KOBRIN PITZELE

Be glad you can suffer, be glad you can feel. . . . How can you tell if you're feeling good unless you've felt bad, so you have something to compare it with?

—THOMAS TRYON

When we are willing to fully experience a particular feeling such as fear, anger, loneliness, or confusion and embrace that emotion without judgment, the blocked energy releases quickly and the feeling dissolves, allowing us to feel more peaceful and open.

—SHAKTI GAWAIN

It's important that you talk about your feelings before they turn into something destructive.

—TOM GALLAGHER

Enthusiasm

Your enthusiasm will be infectious, stimulating and attractive to others. They will love you for it. They will go for you and with you.   —NORMAN VINCENT PEALE

There is a real magic in enthusiasm. It spells the difference between mediocrity and accomplishment. . . . It gives warmth and good feeling to all your personal relationships.   —NORMAN VINCENT PEALE

When a man is willing and eager, the gods join in.
—AESCHYLUS

Enthusiasm is the greatest asset in the world. It beats money and power and influence.   —HENRY CHESTER

So long as enthusiasm lasts, so long is youth still with us.   —DAVID STARR JORDAN

Nothing great was ever achieved without enthusiasm.
—RALPH WALDO EMERSON

Every great and commanding moment in the annals of the world is the triumph of some enthusiasm.
—RALPH WALDO EMERSON

Every calling is great when greatly pursued.
—OLIVER WENDELL HOLMES, JR.

Mere Enthusiasm is the All in All!
—WILLIAM BLAKE

Enthusiasm in maturity—that's the great trick of life.
—DR. FRED PLUM

No person who is enthusiastic about his work has nothing to fear from life. —SAMUEL GOLDWYN

Enthusiasm is the yeast that makes your hopes rise to the stars. Enthusiasm is the sparkle in your eyes, the swing in your gait, the grip of your hand, the irresistible surge of will and energy to execute your ideas.
—HENRY FORD

Nobody grows old merely by a number of years. We grow old by deserting our ideals. Years may wrinkle the skin, but to give up enthusiasm wrinkles the soul.
—SAMUEL ULLMAN

Every man loves what he is good at.
—THOMAS SHADWELL

To business that we love we rise betime,
And go to't with delight.
—SHAKESPEARE

Enthusiasm is the genius of sincerity, and truth accomplishes no victories without it.
—EDWARD GEORGE BULWER-LYTTON

Environment

Healthy people are those who live in healthy homes on a healthy diet in an environment equally fit for birth, growth, work, healing and dying.   —IVAN ILLICH

What is the thing called health? Simply the state in which the individual happens transiently to be perfectly adapted to his environment. Obviously such states cannot be common, for the environment is in constant flux.   —H.L. MENCKEN

A physician is obligated to consider more than a diseased orphan, more even than the whole man—he must view the man in his world.   —ROBERT CECIL

We're living in a very fragile environment. And by the year 2000, we'll fully understand that promoting our health is not just a matter of what we do for our own bodies, but what we do for each other and for the planet.   —LOWELL S. LEVIN

Excess

What a fat belly cost, I wish I had; what it does, I wish
on my enemies.   —Jewish Proverb

A full gorged belly never produced a sprightly mind.
                              —Jeremy Taylor

Gluttony slays more than the sword.
                              —English Proverb

A glutton digs his grave with his teeth.
                              —French Proverb

More die by food than famine.
                              —Thomas Fuller

Gluttony is not a secret vice.
                              —Orson Welles

> O, if a man but knew how many maladies
> Follow from excess and gluttonies,
> He would be more measurable
> In his diet, sitting at his table.
>   —Geoffrey Chaucer

Abundance kills more than hunger.
—GERMAN PROVERB

Many dishes, many diseases.
—LATIN PROVERB

Great eaters and great sleepers are incapable of anything else that is great.   —HENRY IV OF FRANCE

Nothing in excess.
—ENGRAVED BY THE SEVEN WISE MEN, TEMPLE OF APOLLO AT DELPHI

Of all calamities this [excess] is the greatest.
—THOMAS JEFFERSON

Use, do not abuse; neither abstinence nor excess ever renders man happy.   —VOLTAIRE

The case of the total abstainer is worse than that of the overindulger. The second is curable, the first is hopeless.   —CHARLES T. SPRADING

My baseball career surely would have been extended if I didn't indulge myself so much off the field.
—MICKEY MANTLE

Nothing is good in excess, including moderation.
—NANCY WEBER

Too much of a good thing is worse than none at all.
—ENGLISH PROVERB

Too much of a good thing is good for nothing.
—THEODORE HOOK

Too much of a good thing is wonderful.
—MAE WEST

Too much is unhealthy.

—JEWISH PROVERB

Do the best you can, without straining yourself too much and too continuously, and leave the rest to God. If you strain yourself too much you'll have to ask God to patch you up. And for all you know, patching you up may take time that it was planned to use some other way.   —DON MARQUIS

Do it, but don't *over*do it.
—JOSEPH RAYMOND

Exercise

Not less than two hours a day should be devoted to exercise.   —THOMAS JEFFERSON

The Greeks understood that mind and body must develop in harmonious proportion to produce a creative intelligence. And so did the most brilliant intelligence of our earliest day, Thomas Jefferson, when he said, "Not less than two hours a day should be devoted to exercise." If the man who wrote the Declaration of Independence, was Secretary of State and twice President, could give it two hours, our children can give it ten or fifteen minutes.   —JOHN F. KENNEDY

What's the best exercise for reducing? Just move the head slowly from right to left when asked to have a second helping.   —ANONYMOUS

Violent exercise after 40 is especially harmful if you do it with a knife and fork.   —N.E.A. JOURNAL

Those who do not find time for exercise will have to find time for illness.   —OLD PROVERB

Another good reducing exercise consists in placing both hands against the table edge and pushing back.

—ROBERT QUILLEN

I spend up to six hours a day waving my arms about and if everyone did the same thing they would stay much healthier.   —MALCOLM SARGENT, CONDUCTOR.

Exercise has the effect of defusing anger and rage, fear and anxiety. Like music, it soothes the savage in us that lies so close to the surface. It is the ultimate tranquilizer.   —DR. GEORGE SHEEHAN

We live in a time when most people sit a lot—either at a desk, behind a steering wheel or watching television. Our nerves become taut and strained from this sedentary lifestyle. The only way to relieve this stress, this poison that wells up in our bodies, is to do some type of daily exercise.   —JOSEPH SUTTON

Great ideas originate in the muscles.

—THOMAS EDISON

If exercise is neglected, the body will become weak and all its physical powers will be diminished, but with regular exercise the *entire* system will be strengthened and invigorated.   —HARVEY DIAMOND

You cannot exercise only on weekends and satisfy your body's requirements any more than you can eat just on weekends and take care of your nutritional needs.　　　　　—Dr. Harry J. Johnson

Guidelines for Fitness

Frequency: Exercise three to five days a week. Training more than five days a week does not improve cardiorespiratory fitness.

Intensity: Work out 60% to 90% of your heart's maximum pumping capacity. 60% is the minimum level for improved oxygen consumption. To figure that, subtract 220 − 40 (years old, for example) = 180 × .75 (or the desired percentage) = 135 heart beats per minute.

Duration: 15 to 60 minutes of continuous activity.

Mode: Any activity that involves large muscle groups in continuous and rhythmical movement. The exercises recommended are running, walking, hiking, swimming, skating, bicycling, rowing, cross-country skiing and rope skipping.

　　　　　—American College of Sports Medicine

Exercise and temperance can preserve something of our early vigor even in old age.　　　　　—Cicero

Do exercise; for health can no more be had without it.
　　　　　—Brilliana Harley

Exercise is absolutely essential to good health. It's a major key to an energetic, long life.

—Dr. Kenneth H. Cooper

Moderate exercise—even for those in their eighties—reverses many of the effects of aging. For the average older person who does little more than rapid walking for 30 minutes at a time three or four times a week, it can provide 10 years of rejuvenation. Benefits include improved heart and respiratory function, lower blood pressure, increased muscle strength, denser bones, and clearer thinking.

—Researchers at the University of Toronto

Exercise ferments the humors, casts them into their proper channels, throws off redundancies, and helps nature in those secret distributions, without which the body cannot subsist in its vigor, nor the soul act with cheerfulness.   —Joseph Addison

Spend one continuous half an hour, three days a week, on an activity that causes you to breathe a little hard, get your heart rate thumping and break out into a sweat.   —Dr. Ralph Paffenbarger

I take the true definition of exercise to be labor without weariness.   —Samuel Johnson

Definition of a football game: 22 men on the field desperately in need of rest, and 65,000 people in the stands desperately in need of exercise.

—ANONYMOUS

If you do not exercise the body, it corrupts—and the mind corrupts with it.   —BRIAN GLANVILLE

Moderate levels of physical fitness that are attainable by most adults appear to be protective against early mortality.

—INSTITUTE FOR AEROBICS RESEARCH, DALLAS

Increased physical activity leads to improved physical fitness and to other physiological changes. It is the combination of these changes that leads to improved health.   —CENTER FOR DISEASE CONTROL, ATLANTA

Don't lie down when you can sit. Don't sit when you can stand. Don't stand when you can move.

—DR. LAURENCE E. MOREHOUSE

Part of the problem with trying to be fit today is that you have to create a time block every day to exercise. More people may start doing what I've begun doing: getting the exercise in bits and pieces throughout the day instead of all at once.   —EDWARD COYLE

Rosy-complexion'd Health thy steps attends,
And exercise thy lasting youth defends.
—JOHN GAY

If you will form the habit of taking such exercises, you
will see what mighty shoulders you develop, what
sinews, what vigor.　　　　　—EPICTETUS

To cure the mind's wrong bias, Spleen,
Some recommend the bowling green;
Some, hilly walk; all, exercise;
Fling but a stone, the giant dies.
—MATTHEW GREEN

Health is the vital principle of bliss,
And exercise, of health.
—JAMES THOMSON

Unlearn'd, he knew no schoolman's subtle art,
No language, but the language of the heart.
By nature honest, by experience wise,
Healthy by temp'rance, and by exercise.
—ALEXANDER POPE

When I exercise I'm more aware of things.
—GEORGE BRETT

Fanaticism/Obsession

Health nuts are going to feel stupid someday, lying in hospitals dying of nothing.　　　　—RED FOXX

There iz lots ov people in this world who spend so mutch time watching their healths that they hain't got no time to enjoy it.　　　—JOSH BILLINGS (H.W. SHAW)

Those obsessed with health are not healthy; the first requisite of good health is a certain calculated carelessness about oneself.　　　　—SYDNEY J. HARRIS

He destroys his health by laboring to preserve it.
　　　　—VIRGIL

If you mean to keep as well as possible, the less you think about your health the better.
　　　　—OLIVER WENDELL HOLMES, SR.

The truth is that people who worship health cannot remain healthy. —G.K. CHESTERTON

It is the superstition of medicine that is responsible for all the health cults of modern times. You have elevated the desire for health, youth and longevity to the position of a religion. —RABBI STEPHEN S. WISE

People who are always taking care of their health are like misers, who are hoarding up a treasure which they have never spirit enough to enjoy.
—LAURENCE STERNE

Nothing is more fatal to health than the overcare of it.
—BENJAMIN FRANKLIN

It is a grievous illness to preserve one's health by a regimen too strict. —LA ROCHEFOUCAULD

Too much attention to health is a hindrance to learning, to invention and to studies of any kind. . . .
—PLATO

Fasting

Fasting is a medicine.

—St. John Chrysostom

Fasting is better than prayer.

—St. Clement

Fasting today makes the food good tomorrow.

—German Proverb

A fast is better than a bad meal.

—Irish Proverb

Fasting is cleansing, purifying, and restful.

—Meir Schneider

[Juice] Fasting not only accomplishes a physiological regeneration and revitalization of your body, but has a profound stimulating effect on your mental faculties. It also increases your spiritual awareness.

—Paavo Airola

Particularly juice fasting is the most suitable for the purpose of reducing. It keeps hunger to a minimum while it takes inches and pounds off faster than any other reducing regime.   —PAAVO AIROLA

Fasting is the greatest remedy; the physician within.
                              —PHILIPPUS PARACELSUS

Fasting is the most efficient means of correcting any disease.   —DR. ADOLPH MAYER

The elimination of waste products by fasting increases longevity.   —ALEXIS CARREL, M.D.

Nature heals through—fasting—every physical problem that it is possible to heal.   —PAUL C. BRAGG

Make hunger thy sauce, as a medicine for health.
                              —THOMAS TUSSER

I feel like a wisp of cloud, full of light and energy. It's a magical rest for my whole system.   —ANONYMOUS

Once I got rid of the cultural hang-up that I've got to eat all the time, fasting was a snap.   —ANONYMOUS

Fasting is . . . a royal road to healing for anyone who agrees to take it for the recovery and regeneration of the body. —OTTO H.F. BUCHINGER

I now have greater respect for my body's intelligence and capability. Fasting is a marvelous life-lesson.
—ANONYMOUS

One can gain a new perspective on food and one's relationship to it by making fasting part of one's way of life—by fasting at regular intervals, preferably one day each week or three consecutive days in each month.
—DR. ALLAN COTT

The nation badly needs to go on a diet. It should do something drastic about excessive, unattractive, life-threatening fat. It should get rid of it in the quickest way possible—by fasting. —DR. ALLAN COTT

Fasting strengthens control over our appetites, thus contributing to self-mastery. —GEORGE ROMNEY

Fasting cures diseases, dries up bodily humors, puts demons to flight, gets rid of impure thoughts, makes the mind clearer and the heart purer, the body sanctified, and raises man to the throne of God. —ATHENAEUS

If thou woulds't preserve a sound body, use fasting and walking; if a healthful soul, fasting and praying; walking exercises the body, praying exercises the soul, fasting cleanses both.   —FRANCIS QUARLES

A day or two of fasting—quickly clearing the body of nicotine and other toxins—will do most people more good than any amount of medical advice or treatment.
                                        —DR. AGATHA THRASH

It [fasting] can do practically anything. It is a miracle cure. It cured my asthma.   —CLORIS LEACHMAN

Fear

There can be no folly greater than by fearing that which is not.   —ELIZABETH I OF ENGLAND

We must face what we fear; that is the case of the core of the restoration of health.   —MAX LERNER

The only thing we have to fear is fear itself—nameless, unreasoning, unjustified terror which paralyzes needed efforts to convert retreat into advance.
                                        —FRANKLIN D. ROOSEVELT

We should not let our fears hold us back from pursuing our hopes. —JOHN F. KENNEDY

Go fearlessly, not fearfully.

—ANONYMOUS

The greater the fear the nearer the danger.
—DANISH PROVERB

The first duty of man is that of subduing fear.
—THOMAS CARLYLE

The first thing I had to conquer was fear. I realized what a debilitating thing fear is. It can render you absolutely helpless. I know now that fear breeds fear.
—BYRON JANIS

We must constantly build dykes of courage to hold back the flood of fear.   —MARTIN LUTHER KING, JR.

Nothing in life is to be feared. It is only to be understood. —MARIE CURIE

Fear imprisons, faith liberates; fear paralyzes, faith empowers; fear disheartens, faith encourages; fear sickens, faith heals; fear makes useless, faith makes serviceable.   —HARRY EMERSON FOSDICK

We need to learn to take our focus off fears, doubts, worries, and insecurities and place it instead upon faith and a belief that all will work out.   —Amy E. Dean

Why destroy your present happiness by a distant misery, which may never come at all?—for every substantial grief has twenty shadows, and most of the shadows are of your own making.   —Sydney Smith

Real difficulties can be overcome; it is only the imaginary ones that are unconquerable.
     —Theodore N. Vail

The person who fears to try is thus enslaved.
     —Leonard E. Read

Fear is that little darkroom where negatives are developed.   —Michael Pritchard

There is perhaps nothing so bad and so dangerous in life as fear.   —Jawaharlal Nehru

You gain strength, courage and confidence by every experience in which you really stop to look fear in the face. You are able to say to yourself, "I lived through this horror. I can take the next thing that comes along." You must do the thing you think you cannot do.   —Eleanor Roosevelt

Freedom

In health there is freedom. Health is the first of all liberties. —Henri F. Amiel

Health is freedom; sickness is slavery.
—Joseph Sutton

If a man has freedom enough to live healthy, and work at his craft, he has enough. —Goethe

Who then is free? The wise who can command his passions, who fears not want, nor death, nor chains, firmly resisting his appetites and despising the honors of the world, who relies wholly on himself, whose angular points of character have all been rounded off and polished. —Horace

No man is free who is not master of himself.
—Epictetus

I am a free man. I am my own subject to command.
—Anonymous

If you don't run your own life, somebody else will.
—John Atkinson

Your health is bound to be affected if, day by day, you say the opposite of what you feel, if you grovel before what you dislike, and rejoice at what brings you nothing but misfortune. —BORIS PASTERNAK

Freedom is freedom from worry. Having realized that you cannot influence the results, pay no attention to your desires and fears. Let them come and go. Don't give them the nourishment of interest and attention. —NISARGADATTA MAHARAJ

Freedom lies in being bold.

—ROBERT FROST

Bitterness imprisons life; love releases it.
—HARRY EMERSON FOSDICK

I am convinced that we can only learn, grow, create, and change in freedom. —LEO BUSCAGLIA

Friends

Good friends are good for your health.
—DR. IRWIN SARASON

When friends stop being frank and useful to each other, the whole world loses some of its radiance.

—ANATOLE BROYARD

No man is the whole of himself. His friends are the rest of him.

—GOOD LIFE ALMANAC

The man who treasures his friends is usually solid gold himself.

—MARJORIE HOLMES

Friends are relatives you make for yourself.

—EUSTACHE DESCHAMPS

A friend is a person with whom I may be sincere. Before him, I may think aloud.

—RALPH WALDO EMERSON

Be courteous to all, but intimate with few, and let those few be well tried before you give them your confidence. True friendship is a plant of slow growth, and must undergo and withstand the shocks of adversity before it is entitled to the appellation.

—GEORGE WASHINGTON

Good words shall gain you honor in the market-place; but good deeds shall gain you friends among men.

—LAO-TSE

The only way to have a friend is to be one.
—RALPH WALDO EMERSON

Don't lead me; I may not follow. Don't walk behind me; I may not lead. Walk beside me and be my friend.
—ANONYMOUS

A friend is an absolutely phenomenal bit of fortune in one's life.
—BOB RYAN

A real friend is someone who takes a winter vacation on a sun-drenched beach and doesn't send a card.
—FARMER'S ALMANAC

He has no friend who has many friends.
—ARISTOTLE

Blessed are they who have the gift of making friends, for it is one of God's best gifts. It involves many things, but above all, the power of going out of one's self, and appreciating whatever is noble and loving in another.
—THOMAS HUGHES

A friend is a person who is not taken in by sham.
A friend is a person who knows all your faults and doesn't give a damn.
—ANONYMOUS

True friendship is like sound health, the value of it is
seldom known until it is lost.   —C.C. COLTON

A man should keep his friendships in constant repair.
                                        —SAMUEL JOHNSON

Go often to the house of thy friend; for weeds soon
choke up the unused path.   —SCANDINAVIAN PROVERB

If you want to know who your friends are, get yourself a jail sentence.   —CHARLES BUKOWSKI

Being part of a friendly and supportive group of people
is one of the most valuable of all health-building activities. People truly are regenerative for one another.
                                        —ROBERT RODALE

A friend is clearer than the light of heaven, for it would
be better for us that the sun were extinguished than
that we should be without friends.
                                        —ST. JOHN CHRYSOSTOM

Three . . . are my friends: [One] that loves me, [one]
that hates me, [one] that is indifferent to me. Who
loves me, teaches me tenderness. Who hates me,
teaches me caution. Who is indifferent to me, teaches
me self-reliance.   —IVAN PANIN

Friends are those rare people who ask how we are and then wait to hear the answer.   —ED CUNNINGHAM

You can make more friends in two months by becoming interested in other people than you can in two years trying to get other people interested in you.
—DALE CARNEGIE

The character of a man depends on whether he has good or bad friends.   —JAPANESE PROVERB

Let us, then, be what we are, and speak what we think, and in all things keep ourselves loyal to truth and the sacred professions of friendship.
—HENRY WADSWORTH LONGFELLOW

Friendship is almost always the union of a part of one mind with a part of another: People are friends in spots.   —GEORGE SANTAYANA

Gardening

There's a natural method for recapturing youth . . .
the remedy requires no money, physician nor magic.
Just go out in the field and begin to dig and plough.

—GOETHE

When I go into my garden to spade, and dig a bed, I
feel such an exhilaration and health that I discover that
I have been defrauding myself all this time in letting
others do for me what I should have done with my
own hands.   —RALPH WALDO EMERSON

Why do strong arms fatigue themselves with silly
dumb-bells? Trenching a vineyard is worthier exercise
for men.   —MARTIAL

I've always thought it made more sense to use gardening and yard work for exercise rather than pay to go
to a club and pull weights on wires that run through
pulleys. When you finish your garden "workout," you
have accomplished something.   —JOHN P. WILEY, JR.

I got up and went out into the garden to pull weeds for an hour and it was wonderful to feel the whole nervous system quieting down. When I am gardening I do not think of anything at all; I am wholly involved in the physical work and when I go in, I feel whole again, centered.   —MAY SARTON

He who cultivates a garden . . . cultivates and advances at the same time his own nature.
—EZRA WESTON

God Almighty first planned a garden; and indeed it is the purest of human pleasures.   —FRANCIS BACON

Those who labor in the earth are the chosen people of God, if ever he had a chosen people.
—THOMAS JEFFERSON

I want death to find me planting my cabbages.
—MICHEL DE MONTAIGNE

God

I have good health, good thoughts, and good humor, thanks be to God Almighty.   —WILLIAM BYRD

No man is in true health who can not stand in the free air of heaven, with his feet on God's turf, and thank his creator for the simple luxury of physical existence.
—T. W. HIGGINSON

It is only by forgetting yourself that you draw near to God. —HENRY DAVID THOREAU

He who desires to see the living God face to face should not seek Him in the empty firmament of his mind, but in human love. —FEODOR DOSTOEVSKY

What we are is God's gift to us. What we become is our gift to God. —LOUIS NIZER

God grant me the serenity to accept the things
    I cannot change,
the courage to change the things I can,
And the wisdom to know the difference.
—ALCOHOLICS ANONYMOUS PRAYER

The best medicine I know for Rheumatism is to thank the Lord it ain't the gout.
—JOSH BILLINGS (H.W. SHAW)

God made the human body, and it is by far the most exquisite and wonderful organization which has come to us from the Divine hand.
—HENRY WARD BEECHER

I do look up and communicate lovingly with my friend up there . . . although I know God is within. I look up and laugh and live. —MARY MARTIN

God heals, and the doctor takes the fee.
—BENJAMIN FRANKLIN

I really think the Universe, or God, or whatever you want to call it, does the healing. I just collect the fee.
—DR. RICHARD DIAMOND

I dressed him; God cured him.
—AMBROISE PARÉ

We cannot go where God is not, and where God is, all is well. —ANONYMOUS

Have courage for the great sorrows of life and patience for the small ones; and when you have laboriously accomplished your daily task, go to sleep in peace. God is awake. —VICTOR HUGO

The Good Life

To find the good life you must become yourself.
—Dr. Bill Jackson

There are three ingredients in the good life: learning, earning and yearning.   —Christopher Morley

The good life is to live on honorable terms with your own soul.   —Saul Bellow

A long life lived is not good enough, but a good life lived is long enough.   —Bernard Jensen

Do not worry; eat three square meals a day; say your prayers; be courteous to your creditors; keep your digestion good; exercise; go slow and easy. Maybe there are other things your special case requires to make you happy but, my friend, these I reckon will give you a good life.
—Attributed to Abraham Lincoln

Growth/Progress

Be not afraid of growing slowly, be afraid only of standing still.   —CHINESE PROVERB

The only real satisfaction there is, is to be growing up inwardly all the time, becoming more just, true, generous, simple, manly, womanly, kind, active. And this can we all do, by doing each day the day's work as well as we can.   —JAMES FREEMAN CLARKE

We must always change, renew, rejuvenate ourselves; otherwise we harden.   —GOETHE

There's always room for improvement—it's the biggest room in the house.   —LOUISE HEATH LEBER

Behold the turtle. He makes progress only when he sticks his neck out.   —JAMES B. CONANT

The dark or sick days need not be seen as bad days, for they often prompt our deepest reflection and, in some cases, a change of life-style. In this sense, then, one can look upon darkness or disease not as an end but as a beginning of growth.
                    —EILEEN ROCKEFELLER GROWALD

It used to be that when something happened to me like it did Monday night I'd get down. I used to take things home and let them bother me. But last year I came to realize when it's gone, it's gone. There's nothing I can do about it after it's past. You're not helping yourself or the team getting down. So, Monday night I had a beer, recapped what I had done and then forgot about it.
—WILL CLARK

It is necessary to try to surpass oneself always; this occupation ought to last as long as life.
—CHRISTINA, QUEEN OF SWEDEN

Soul growth is most important of all for developing the higher nature of man. I believe the inner man is most important to take care of.
—BERNARD JENSEN

It is in living wisely and fully that one's soul grows.
—A.H. COMPTON

We find comfort among those who agree with us—growth among those who don't.
—FRANK A. CLARK

You grow up the day you have the first real laugh—at yourself.
—ETHEL BARRYMORE

There are as many ways to live and grow as there are people. Our own ways are the only ways that should matter to us.
—EVELYN MANDEL

We've discovered that our growth today depends upon our mental, physical, and spiritual health. If we picture these three as the legs of a stool, we can see that shortchanging the importance of one or taking one of them away will upset the balance.

—AMY E. DEAN

There is no royal road to anything. One thing at a time, all things in succession. That which grows fast withers as rapidly; that which grows slowly endures.

—J.G. HOLLAND

He who ceases to grow greater becomes smaller.

—HENRI F. AMIEL

All that is human must retrograde if it does not advance.

—EDWARD GIBBON

Disease is very old, and nothing about it has changed. It is we who change, as we learn to recognize what was formerly imperceptible. —JEAN MARTIN CHARCOT

Happiness

Happiness is good health and a bad memory.
—INGRID BERGMAN

The greatest happiness you can have is knowing that you do not necessarily require happiness.
—WILLIAM SAROYAN

Health is the ground-work for all happiness.
—LEIGH HUNT

Our greatest happiness does not depend on the condition of life in which chance has placed us, but is always the result of a good conscience, good health, occupation, and freedom in all just pursuits.
—THOMAS JEFFERSON

Happiness is not being pained in body nor troubled in mind.
—THOMAS JEFFERSON

If the word happiness means anything, it means an inner feeling of well-being, a sense of balance, a feeling of being contented with life. These can exist only when one feels free. —A.S. Neill

Get happiness out of your work or you may never know what happiness is. —Elbert Hubbard

Storybook happiness involves every form of pleasant thumb-twiddling; true happiness involves the full use of one's powers and talents. —John W. Gardner

Happiness isn't something you experience; it's something you remember. —Oscar Levant

The moments of happiness we enjoy take us by surprise. It is not that we seize them, but that they seize us. —Ashley Montagu

Now and then it's good to pause in our pursuit of happiness and just be happy. —Anonymous

In the pursuit of happiness, the difficulty lies in knowing when you have caught up. —R.H. Grenville

There can be no happiness if the things we believe in are different from the things we do. —Freya Stark

The grand essentials to happiness in this life are something to do, something to love and something to hope for.   —JOSEPH ADDISON

Be happy. It is a way of being wise.
                                              —COLETTE

Happiness is the meaning and the purpose of life, the whole aim and end of human existence.
                                              —ARISTOTLE

Where ambition ends happiness begins.
                                              —HUNGARIAN PROVERB

Most people ask for happiness on condition. Happiness can only be felt if you don't set any condition.
                                              —ARTUR RUBINSTEIN

Happiness comes of the capacity to feel deeply, to enjoy simply, to think freely, to risk life, to be needed.
                                              —STORM JAMESON

The only way on earth to multiply happiness is to divide it.   —PAUL SCHERER

That is happiness: to be dissolved into something complete and great. When it comes to one, it comes as naturally as sleep.   —WILLA CATHER

Remember this—that very little is needed to make a happy life. —MARCUS AURELIUS

If you want to be happy, be.
—LEO TOLSTOY

It is not what we see and touch or that which others do for us which makes us happy; it is that which we think and feel and do, first for the other fellow and then for ourselves. —HELEN KELLER

Even a happy life cannot be without a measure of darkness, and the word "happiness" would lose its meaning if it were not balanced by sadness. —CARL JUNG

To be happy means to be free, not from pain or fear, but from care or anxiety. —W.H. AUDEN

Such happiness as life is capable of comes from the full participation of all our powers in the endeavor to wrest from each changing situation of experience its own full and unique meaning. —JOHN DEWEY

What is your happiness worth when you have to strive and labor for it? True happiness is spontaneous and effortless. —NISARGADATTA MAHARAJ

To give happiness is to deserve happiness.
—CHINESE FORTUNE COOKIE

Happy people do not get sick as often as sad ones. In fact, people who become depressed and discouraged by the problems of life are already half-sick just by their attitude. —SUN BEAR

A person must be happy to be well and be well to be happy. —BERNARD JENSEN

Happiness: a good bank account, a good cook and a good digestion. —JEAN JACQUES ROUSSEAU

Give a man health and a course to steer, and he'll never stop to trouble about whether he's happy or not. —GEORGE BERNARD SHAW

Be happy while y'er leevin,
For y'er a lang time deid.
—SCOTTISH PROVERB

It is not how much we have, but how much we enjoy, that makes happiness. —C.H. SPURGEON

Happiness comes from striving—doing—loving—conquering—always something positive and forceful. —DAVID STARR JORDAN

We are happy when, however briefly, we become one with ourselves, others and the world of nature. —DAVID COLE GORDON

If one only wished to be happy, this could be easily accomplished; but we wish to be happier than other people, and this is always difficult, for we believe others to be happier than they are. —MONTESQUIEU

If you ever find happiness by hunting for it, you will find it as the old woman did her lost spectacles, safe on her own nose all the time.
—JOSH BILLINGS (H.W. SHAW)

Happiness grows at our own firesides, and it is not to be picked up in strangers' gardens.
—DOUGLAS JERROLD

Happiness lies, first of all, in health.
—GEORGE WILLIAM CURTIS

All happiness depends on a leisurely breakfast.
—JOHN GUNTHER

Happiness may well consist primarily of an attitude toward time. —ROBERT GRUDIN

The secret of happiness is to find a congenial monotony. —V.S. PRITCHETT

Act as if you were already happy and that will tend to make you happy. —DALE CARNEGIE

For the happiest life, days should be rigorously planned, nights left open to chance.
—MIGNON MCLAUGHLIN

The hours that make us happy make us wise.
—JOHN MASEFIELD

Remember that happiness is a way of travel—not the destination.
—ROY M. GOODMAN

If we're happy, we're exploring. If we're unhappy, we're resisting.
—DEAN BLACK

Health

One must have health! You may banish money—banish sofas—banish wine! but right Jack Health, true Jack Health, honest Jack Health—banish health, and you banish all the world!
—ANNE CRAWFORD FLEXNER

Health is a precious thing, and the only one, in truth, meriting that a man should lay out, not only his time, sweat, labor and goods, but also his life itself to obtain it.
—MICHEL DE MONTAIGNE

Your health comes first—you can always hang yourself later.   —Jewish Proverb

Life is not merely to be alive, but to be well.
                                    —Martial

Health is what matters almost most.
                                    —Bob Ryan

O blessed health! . . . thou art above all gold and treasure . . . .He that has thee, has little more to wish for;
and he that is so wretched as to want thee, wants
everything with thee.   —Laurence Sterne

Health, eldest of gods, with thee may I dwell for the
rest of my life!   —Ariphon the Sicyonian

Without health, life is not life; life is lifeless.
                              —Ariphon the Sicyonian

Take care of health; for without it, existence is, for
every purpose of enjoyment, worse than a blank.
                              —Emma Hart Willard

O health! health! the blessing of the rich! the riches of
the poor! who can buy thee at too dear a rate, since
there is no enjoying this world without thee?
                                    —Ben Jonson

Health is the first good lent to men;
A gentle disposition then;
Next, to be rich by no by-ways;
Lastly, with friends t' enjoy our days.
—ROBERT HERRICK

There is no joy even in beautiful Wisdom, unless one has holy Health. —SIMONIDES

Pay attention to the most important thing of all, the care of your health. —CATO

If health be yours, you have more than enough. —CATO

If all be well with belly, feet, and sides,
A king's estate no greater good provides.
—HORACE

Health is the greatest of all possessions; a pale cobbler is better than a sick king. —ISAAC BICKERSTAFF

There is nothing in life that is as important as life, as health. —JOSEPH RAYMOND

Health is the soul that animates all the enjoyments of life, which fade and are tasteless without it.
—WILLIAM TEMPLE

To lose one's health renders science null, art inglorious, strength unavailing, wealth useless, and elegance powerless.   —Herophilus

Health is the natural state of equilibrium to which all individuals, society, and nature aspire.
                    —Eileen Rockefeller Growald

Health is not everything, but without health, everything else is nothing.   —Bernard Jensen

Health is when all systems are go.
                    —Dr. Richard Diamond

Health is a living response to one's total environment.
                    —Dr. Bob Hoke

Health is man adapting, man striving, man living the present and thrusting himself into the future.
                    —Dr. George Sheehan

A wise man ought to realize that health is his most valuable possession.   —Hippocrates

The health of a people is really the foundation upon which all their happiness and all their power as a State depend.   —Benjamin Disraeli

Health is the primary duty of life.

—OSCAR WILDE

Healthy citizens are the greatest asset any country can have. —WINSTON CHURCHILL

Heart Disease

Many a man who would not dream of putting too much pressure in his automobile tires lays a constant overstrain on his heart and arteries.

—BRUCE BARTON

We are a divided species—head running ahead of heart. It is no surprise that coronary thrombosis is the characteristic death of our time. The heart literally chokes up on the impossibility of keeping up.

—BRIAN ALDISS

All American males are candidates for heart disease— now generally recognized as the greatest health threat in any industrialized society. And overweight, lack of exercise, high blood pressure, smoking and a high cholesterol increase their chance of having a heart attack by 10 times. —DR. GEORGE SHEEHAN

The trouble with heart disease is that the first symptom is often hard to deal with: instant death.

—MICHAEL PHELPS, M.D.

You don't have to exercise so vigorously to get an aerobic effect. Even moderate activity like working around the house can reduce your risk of heart disease.

—DR. KENNETH H. COOPER

There's so much evidence associating inactivity with heart disease that it's almost beyond question.

—DR. KENNETH H. COOPER

Helping Others

In nothing do men more nearly approach the gods than in doing good to their fellow men.   —CICERO

The only ones among you who will be really happy are those who will have sought and found how to serve.

—ALBERT SCHWEITZER

To live is not to live for oneself alone; let us help one another.   —MENANDER

We are here to help each other, to try to make each other happy.   —Polar Eskimo Saying

Goodness is the only investment that never fails.
                                —Henry David Thoreau

It is one of the most beautiful compensations of this life that no man can sincerely try to help another without helping himself.   —Ralph Waldo Emerson

My country is the world and my religion is to do good.
                                —Thomas Paine

No one is useless in this world who lightens the burden of it to anyone else.   —Charles Dickens

No man is an Island, intire of it selfe; every man is a peece of the Continent, a part of the maine; if a Clod bee washed away by the Sea, Europe is the lesse, as well as if a Promontorie were, as well as if a Manner of thy friends or of thine owne were; any man's death diminishes me, because I am involved in Mankinde; and therefore never send to know for whom the bell tolls: It tolls for thee.   —John Donne

To be happy you must forget yourself. Learn benevolence; it is the only cure of a morbid temper.
                                —Edward George Bulwer-Lytton

Help thy brother's boat across, and lo! thine own has
reached the shore.   —HINDU PROVERB

To be of use in the world is the only way to be happy.
                    —HANS CHRISTIAN ANDERSEN

Only the life in the service of others is worth living.
                    —ALBERT EINSTEIN

You will find, as you look back upon your life, that the
moments that stand out are the moments when you
have done things for others.   —HENRY DRUMMOND

The greatest object in the universe, says a certain
philosopher, is a good man struggling with adversity;
yet there is a still greater, which is the good man that
comes to relieve it.   —OLIVER GOLDSMITH

Good will is the mightiest practical force in the
universe.   —CHARLES FLETCHER DOLE

Holistic Medicine

Natural forces are the healers of disease.
                    —HIPPOCRATES

Disease has social as well as physical, chemical, and biological causes. —HENRY E. SIEGRIST

The human body is like a bakery with a thousand windows. We are looking into only one window of the bakery when we are investigating one particular aspect of a disease. —BÉLA SCHICK

The cure of many diseases is unknown to the physicians of Hellas, because they are ignorant of the whole, which ought to be studied also; for the part can never be well unless the whole is well. —PLATO

Body and soul cannot be separated for purposes of treatment, for they are one and indivisible. Sick minds must be healed as well as sick bodies.
—C. JEFF MILLER

Knowledge indeed is a desirable, a lovely possession, but I do not scruple to say that health is more so. It is of little consequence to store the mind with science if the body be permitted to become debilitated. If the body be feeble, the mind will not be strong.
—THOMAS JEFFERSON

Diet, exercise, stress reduction, social support, meditation, imagery, and attitudinal factors can play an important role in maximizing the quality of life for people with cancer and other chronic illnesses.
—MICHAEL LERNER
—RACHEL NAOMI REMEN

The holistic philosophy is to nurture and nourish the entire being—the Body, the Mind, and the Spirit. If we ignore any of these areas, we are incomplete, we lack wholeness. —LOUISE L. HAY

In a holistic approach that integrates techniques ranging from meditation to the most modern technology lies a new medicine that seeks a balance within ourselves and with our environment. —KENNETH R. PELLETIER

To resist the frigidity of old age one must combine the body, the mind and the heart—and to keep them in parallel vigor one must exercise, study and love. —KARL VON BONSTETTEN

The body must be repaired and supported, if we would preserve the mind in all its vigor. —PLINY THE YOUNGER

Complete health and awakening are really the same. —TARTHANG TULKU

I would hope that it will become clearer to everyone that the purpose of healing is to bring us in harmony with our earth, with our environment, and with ourselves. —O. CARL SIMONTON

Health necessarily involves the coordination and congruence of all aspects of one's being, including communications and relationships with others and with the environment. It embraces every aspect of life, including diet, exercise, work, play, and relaxation.
—EMMETT E. MILLER

Healing does not necessarily mean to become physically well or to be able to get up and walk around again. Rather, it means achieving a balance between the physical, emotional, intellectual, and spiritual dimensions.
—ELISABETH KÜBLER-ROSS

Healing is a total, organismic, synergistic response that must emerge from within the individual if recovery and growth are to be accomplished.
—JANET F. QUINN

One of the basic principles of holistic health is that we cannot separate our physical body from our emotional, mental, and spiritual states of being. For instance, when we have a physical disorder, it is a message for us to look deeply into our emotional and intuitive feelings, our thoughts and attitudes, to discover how we need to take better care of ourselves emotionally, mentally, or spiritually, as well as physically. With this approach, we can restore the natural harmony and balance within our being.
—SHAKTI GAWAIN

The medical school of the future will concentrate its efforts upon bringing about that harmony between body, mind and soul which results in the relief and cure of disease.   —DR. EDWARD BACH

Hope

He who has health has hope, and he who has hope has everything.   —ARABIAN PROVERB

While there is life there is hope.

                    —CICERO

In adversity, man is saved by hope.

                    —MENANDER

In the hour of adversity be not without hope,
For crystal rain falls from black clouds.
                    —NEZAMI

Hope is the thing with feathers
    That perches in the soul,
And sings the tune without the words,
    And never stops at all.
                    —EMILY DICKINSON

In spite of everything I still believe that people are really good at heart. I simply can't build up my hopes on a foundation consisting of confusion, misery, and death. I see the world gradually being turned into a wilderness, I hear the ever approaching thunder, which will destroy us too, I can feel the sufferings of millions and yet, if I look up into the heavens, I think that it will all come right, that this cruelty too will end, and that peace and tranquility will return again.

—ANNE FRANK

Hope is the dream of a waking man.

—DIOGENES

We have no right to have no hope, because if we have no hope, there is no hope. The basic ethics for modern man conscious of what humanity is running into is to firmly stick to the will of doing something about it and therefore the belief that something can be done about it. —JACQUES MONOD

Without humor there is no hope, and man could no more live without hope than he could without the earth underfoot. —WILLIAM SAROYAN

There is no such thing as false hope . . . .If statistics say that 9 out of 10 people die from a disease, I tell my patient, "You can be the one who gets well."

—DR. BERNIE SIEGEL

Hope is the only bee that makes honey without flowers.   —ROBERT INGERSOLL

Hope is the physician of each misery.
                                    —IRISH PROVERB

Confidence and hope do more good than physic.
                                    —GALEN

Hope is necessary in every condition. The miseries of poverty, sickness, of captivity, would, without this comfort, be insupportable.   —SAMUEL JOHNSON

In the midst of winter, I finally learned that there was in me an invincible summer.   —ALBERT CAMUS

I believe that if things don't turn out the way I want, it's because there's a better way up ahead.
                                    —ANONYMOUS

The hopeful man sees success where others see failure, sunshine where others see shadows and storm.
                                    —O.S. MARDEN

It has never been, and never will be, easy work! But the road that is built in hope is more pleasant to the traveler than the road built in despair, even though they both lead to the same destination.
                                    —MARIAN ZIMMER BRADLEY

You believe that easily which you hope for earnestly.

—TERENCE

The miserable have no other medicine
But only hope.

—SHAKESPEARE

Know then, whatever cheerful and serene
Supports the mind, supports the body too;
Hence, the most vital movement mortals feel
Is hope, the balm and lifeblood of the soul.

—JOHN ARMSTRONG

We must accept finite disappointment, but we must
never lose infinite hope.   —MARTIN LUTHER KING, JR.

We live by our genius for hope; we survive by our
talent for dispensing with it.   —V.S. PRITCHETT

Just as despair can come to one only from other human
beings, hope, too, can be given to one only by other
human beings.   —ELIE WIESEL

Humor/Laughter

A sense of humor is the ability to understand a joke—
and that the joke is oneself.   —CLIFTON FADIMAN

Humor is such a strong weapon, such a strong answer.
                                       —AGNES VARDA

Humor—the ability to laugh at life—is right at the top,
with love and communication, in the hierarchy of our
needs. Humor has much to do with pain; it exaggerates
the anxieties and absurdities we feel, so that we gain
distance and, through laughter, relief.
                                       —SARA DAVIDSON

On life's journey from diaper rash to Polygrip, humor
is the best pain reliever.   —NANCY MCINTYRE

The only thing worth having in an earthly existence is
a sense of humor.   —LINCOLN STEFFENS

Every survival kit should include a sense of humor.
                                       —ANONYMOUS

Good-humor and gay spirits are the liberators, the sure
cure for spleen and melancholy.   —A.B. ALCOTT

True humor springs not more from the head than from the heart; it is not contempt, its essence is love; it issues not in laughter, but in still smiles, which lie far deeper. —THOMAS CARLYLE

He who laughs, lasts.
—MARY PETTIBONE POOLE

Laughter makes good blood.
—ITALIAN PROVERB

Laughter is a form of internal jogging. It moves your internal organs around. It enhances respiration. It is an igniter of great expectations. —NORMAN COUSINS

Laughter is wine for the soul—laughter soft, or loud and deep, tinged through with seriousness . . . .the hilarious declaration made by man that life is worth living. —SEAN O'CASEY

Laughter is a tranquilizer with no side effects.
—ARNOLD H. GLASOW

Laughter is the sun that drives winter from the human face. —VICTOR HUGO

Laughter is the only thing that'll cut trouble down to a size where you can talk to it. —DAN JENKINS

Always laugh when you can. It is cheap medicine.

—Lord Byron

The most wasted of all our days are those in which we have not laughed.　—Nicolas Chamfort

If you don't learn to laugh at trouble, you won't have anything to laugh at when you grow old.

—Ed Howe

The sound of laughter has always seemed to me the most civilized music in the universe.

—Peter Ustinov

He deserves Paradise who makes his companions laugh.　—Mohammed

For me, a hearty belly laugh is one of the beautiful sounds in the world.　—Bennett Cerf

Laughter has no foreign accent.

—Paul B. Lowney

Have you ever had a depressing thought in the middle of a good laugh?　—Douglas Bloch

If you are wise, laugh.

—Martial

In laughter there is always a kind of joyousness that is incompatible with contempt or indignation.

—VOLTAIRE

Laugh at yourself first, before anybody else can.

—ELSA MAXWELL

Live merrily as thou canst, for by honest mirth we cure many passions of the mind.   —ROBERT BURTON

I live in a constant endeavor to fence against the infirmities of ill health, and other evils of life, by mirth.

—LAURENCE STERNE

A man without mirth is like a wagon without springs, in which one is caused disagreeably to jolt by every pebble over which it runs.   —HENRY WARD BEECHER

Comedy is medicine.

—TREVOR GRIFFITHS

Idleness

He that is busy is tempted by but one devil; he that is idle, by a legion. —THOMAS FULLER

Idleness is the Devil's pillow.

—DANISH PROVERB

Expect poison from standing water.

—WILLIAM BLAKE

He dies every day who lives a lingering life.

—PIERRARD POULLET

Doing nothing is doing ill.

—JAPANESE PROVERB

I like work; it fascinates me. I can sit and look at it for hours. I love to keep it by me; the idea of getting rid of it nearly breaks my heart. —JEROME K. JEROME

The hardest work of all is to do nothing.
—JEWISH PROVERB

One monster there is in the world: the idle man.
—THOMAS CARLYLE

It is impossible to enjoy idling thoroughly unless one has plenty of work to do.   —JEROME K. JEROME

Idleness is the refuge of weak minds, and the holiday of fools.   —LORD CHESTERFIELD

Mind unemployed is mind unenjoyed.
—C.N. BOVEE

The secret of being miserable is to have the leisure to bother about whether you are happy or not.
—GEORGE BERNARD SHAW

Idleness is the root of all evil.
—GEORGE FARQUHAR

Idleness is the mother of vices.
—JOHN LYDGATE

Without business, debauchery.
—GEORGE HERBERT

Imagination

We go to the beach
I look at the sea
My mother thinks I stare
My father thinks I want to go in the water.
But I have my own little world.
—AMY LEVY, 12-YEARS-OLD

Imagination has always had powers of resurrection
that no science can match.   —INGRID BENGIS

Imagination is more important than knowledge.
—ALBERT EINSTEIN

To know is nothing at all; to imagine is everything.
—ANATOLE FRANCE

The first of our senses which we should take care
never to let rust through disuse is that sixth sense, the
imagination . . . .I mean the wide-open eye which
leads us always to see truth more vividly, to apprehend
more broadly, to concern ourselves more deeply, to
be, all our life long, sensitive and awake to the powers
and responsibilities given to us as human beings.
—CHRISTOPHER FRY

If you can imagine it, you can achieve it.
If you can dream it, you can become it.
—William Arthur Ward

Imagination is not a talent of some men but is the health of every man. —Ralph Waldo Emerson

The use of the imagination is a wonderful blessing if you will use it. You will become happier, more enlightened, alive, impassioned, light-hearted and generous to everybody else. Even your health will improve. Colds will disappear and all the other ailments of discouragement and boredom. —Brenda Ueland

Imagination nurtures human reality as a river brings life to a desert. —Martin L. Rossman, M.D.

The world of reality has its limits; the world of imagination is boundless. —Jean Jacques Rousseau

In the world of imagination, all things belong.
—Richard Hugo

The great instrument of moral good is the imagination.
—Percy Bysshe Shelley

Imagination is the eye of the soul.
—Joseph Joubert

Using your imagination is like exercising. It feels so good after you do it. —JUDITH LEVY-SENDER

Indecision

Nothing is so exhausting as indecision, and nothing is so futile. —BERTRAND RUSSELL

I dislike indecision. I prefer to make a mistake than to do nothing. If you make a mistake you at least have the mistake, you can study it, and you can even expect to avoid making a similar mistake the next time that kind of situation comes up. —WILLIAM SAROYAN

There is grief in indecision.

—CICERO

I must have a prodigious quantity of mind; it takes me as much as a week, sometimes, to make it up.

—MARK TWAIN

What the hell—you might be right, you might be wrong . . . but don't just *avoid*.

—KATHARINE HEPBURN

Inner Strength

What lies behind us and what lies before us are tiny matters compared to what lies within us.
— RALPH WALDO EMERSON

We can be sure that the greatest hope for maintaining equilibrium in the face of any situation rests within ourselves. Persons who are secure with a transcendental system of values and deep sense of moral duties are possessors of values which no man and no catastrophe can take from him.   — DR. RANCIS J. BRACELAND

I don't believe in political movements. I believe in personal movement of the soul when a man who looks at himself is so ashamed that he tries to make some sort of change—within himself, not on the outside.
— JOSEPH BRODSKY

When a person is depressed or confused, the physician's advice is just one part of the prescription for spiritual renewal. The patient needs to learn to look within to find his or her own strength. It's like dancing. You can't learn to dance by listening to someone explain it to you; you have to get up and do it.
— CARL HAMMERSCHLAG, M.D.

My strength is as the strength of ten,
Because my heart is pure.
—Lord Tennyson

Look well into thyself; there is a source of strength which will always spring up if thou wilt always look there. —Marcus Aurelius

To live happily is an inward power of the soul.
—Marcus Aurelius

The strength you've insisted on assigning to others is actually within yourself. —Lisa Alther

Serenity comes not alone by removing the outward causes and occassions of fear, but by the discovery of inward reservoirs to draw upon. —Rufus M. Jones

Inner Voice

It's supposed to be a professional secret, but I'll tell you anyway. We doctors do nothing. We only help and encourage the doctor within.
—Albert Schweitzer

If you can get back in tune with your body, it will tell you what it wants. One way of doing that is to start to have more faith and confidence in your own instincts, logic, and common sense.   —HARVEY DIAMOND

In order to heal themselves, people must recognize, first, that they have an inner guidance deep within and, second, that they can trust it.
                                        —SHAKTI GAWAIN

When we are trying to decide what to do, or when we are not quite certain what we really want, we can usually find the answer just by tuning in to our inner wisdom . . . .Once we can contact that inner guide, we need only ask ourselves, "What feels right to me? What do I really want? What is true for me at this moment? Where is my energy taking me right now?"
                                        —SHAKTI GAWAIN

I learned that nothing is impossible when we follow our inner guidance, even when its direction may threaten us by reversing our logic.
                                        —GERALD JAMPOLSKY

Journey/Travel

It is good to have an end to journey towards; but it is the journey that matters, in the end.

—URSULA K. LEGUIN

If you look like your passport photo, in all probability you need the journey.   —EARL WILSON

Of journeying the benefits are many; the freshness it brings to the heart, the seeing and hearing of marvelous things, the delight of beholding new cities, the meeting of unknown friends, the learning of high manners.   —SAADI

The journey of a thousand miles begins with one step.

—LAO-TSE

Afoot and light-hearted I take to the open road,
Healthy, free, the world before me,
The long brown path before me leading wherever I
  choose.
Henceforth I ask not good-fortune, I myself am
  good-fortune,
Henceforth I whimper no more, postpone no more,
  need nothing,
Done with indoor complaints, libraries, querulous
  criticisms,
Strong and content I travel the open road.

—WALT WHITMAN

I hit the open road, the good old open road where you
don't have time to think of the past or future, the road
where everything is always different and fresh, the
road where you have to use every one of your senses,
the road, in short, that makes you live in the present.

—JOSEPH RAYMOND

I am much pleased that you are going on a very long
journey, which may by proper conduct restore your
health and prolong your life. Observe these rule:

1. Turn all care out of your head as soon as you mount
    the chaise.
2. Do not think about frugality; your health is worth
    more than it can cost.
3. Do not continue any day's journey to fatigue.
4. Take now and then a day's rest.
5. Cast away all anxiety, and keep your mind easy.

—SAMUEL JOHNSON

The soul of a journey is liberty, perfect liberty, to think, feel, do, just as one pleases.

—WILLIAM HAZLITT

He who would travel happily must travel light.

—ANTOINE DE SAINT-EXUPÉRY

The truth is, I am traveling for my health, and therefore I am taking cross-roads, and stopping at out of the way places. For there is no health to be got by staying in cities, and putting up at crowded hotels, and accepting invitations to dinner-parties and tea-parties, or in doing any thing else that is fashionable.

—ELIZA LESLIE

Travel teaches toleration.

—BENJAMIN DISRAELI

Whenever I find myself growing grim about the mouth; whenever it is a damp, drizzly November in my soul; whenever I find myself involuntarily pausing before coffin warehouses, and bringing up the rear of every funeral I meet; and especially whenever my hypos get such an upper hand of me, that it requires a strong moral principle to prevent me from deliberately stepping into the street, and methodically knocking people's hats off—then I account it high time to get to sea as soon as I can.   —HERMAN MELVILLE

I travel not to go anywhere, but to go. I travel for travel's sake. The great affair is to move.

—ROBERT LOUIS STEVENSON

No man needs a vacation so much as the person who has just had one. —ELBERT HUBBARD

Kindness

One of the most difficult things to give away is kindness—it is usually returned.   —CORT R. FLINT

The greatness of a man can nearly always be measured by his willingness to be kind.   —G. YOUNG

Kindness is the golden chain by which society is bound together.   —GOETHE

Kindness is the beginning and end of the law.
        —HEBREW PROVERB

Kindness is a language the deaf can hear and the dumb can understand.   —ANONYMOUS

There is a magnet in your heart that will attract true friends. That magnet is unselfishness, thinking of others first.   —PARAMAHANSA YOGANANDA

Little deeds of kindness, little words of love,
Help to make earth happy like the Heaven above.
                              —JULIA FLETCHER CARNEY

Do unto others as though you were others.
                              —ANONYMOUS

How beautiful a day can be when kindness touches it.
                              —GEORGE ELLISTON

Kindness in words creates confidence.
Kindness in thinking creates profoundness.
Kindness in giving creates love.
                              —LAO-TSE

Kindness can become its own motive. We are made
kind by being kind.   —ERIC HOFFER

Kindness is like a beautiful flowering plant. Pay attention to it, water it, nourish it, tend to its needs, and it
will flourish. . . . Show it no kindness, and it will close
up its beauty and die.   —AMY E. DEAN

It would all be so beautiful if people were just
kind . . . what is more wise than to be kind? And what
is more kind than to understand?   —THOMAS TRYON

No act of kindness, however small, is ever wasted.
                              —DOUGLAS BLOCH

Life is short and we never have enough time for gladdening the hearts of those who travel the way with us. O, be swift to love! Make haste to be kind.

—HENRI F. AMIEL

I have wept in the night
For the shortness of sight
That to somebody's need made me blind;
But I have never yet
Felt a tinge of regret
For being a little too kind.

—ANONYMOUS

That best portion of a good man's life,
His little, nameless, unremembered acts
Of kindness and of love.

—WILLIAM WORDSWORTH

If you cannot lift the load off another's back, do not walk away. Try to lighten it.   —FRANK TYGER

I shall pass through this world but once. If, therefore, there be any kindness I can show, or any good thing I can do, let me do it now. Let me not defer it or neglect it, for I shall not pass this way again.

—WILLIAM PENN

Two important things are to have a genuine interest in people and to be kind to them. Kindness, I've discovered, is everything in life.

—ISAAC BASHEVIS SINGER

Knowledge/Learning

There is a time in every man's education when he arrives at the conviction that envy is ignorance; that imitation is suicide; that he must take himself, for better or for worse, as his portion; that, though the wide universe is full of good, no kernel of nourishing corn can come to him but through his toil bestowed on that plot of ground which is given him to till.

—Ralph Waldo Emerson

Our present education is rotten because it teaches us to love success and not what we are doing. The result has become more important than the action.

—J. Krishnamurti

Interest and attention will insure to you an education.

—Robert A. Millikan

The direction in which education starts a man will determine his future life.   —Plato

Every man who rises above the common level has received two educations: the first from his teachers; the second, more personal and important, from himself.   —Edward Gibbon

I have never let my schooling interfere with my education.   —Mark Twain

Education is a social process . . . .Education is growth . . . .Education is not preparation for life; education is life itself.   —John Dewey

Education's purpose is to replace an empty mind with an open one.   —Malcolm S. Forbes

There is still an immense amount to be learned about health, but if what is at present known to a few were part of the general knowledge, the average expectation of life could probably be increased by about ten years.
                          —John B.S. Haldane

As knowledge with regard to the effects of food upon man increases, it is more than conceivable that the races that first avail themselves of the new values of nutrition may decrease the handicaps of disease, lengthen their lives, and so become the leaders of the future.   —Victor G. Heiser

You know more than you think you do.
                          —Dr. Benjamin Spock

A little knowledge is a dangerous thing, but a little want of knowledge is also a dangerous thing.
                          —Samuel Butler

A good listener is not only popular everywhere, but after a while he knows something.
—WILSON MIZNER

They know enough who know how to learn.
—HENRY ADAMS

No knowledge can be more satisfactory to a man than that of his own frame, its parts, their functions and actions.
—THOMAS JEFFERSON

So much one man can do that does both act and know.
—ANDREW MARVELL

Knowledge, in truth, is the great sun in the firmament. Life and power are scattered with all its beams.
—DANIEL WEBSTER

When you're through learning, you're through.
—VERNON LAW

One remains young as long as one can still learn, can still take on new habits, can bear contradictions.
—MARIE VON EBNER-ESCHENBACH

The more I learn, the more enjoyable life becomes.
—SOL SENDER

Learning is a treasure which accompanies its owner everywhere. —CHINESE PROVERB

That is what learning is. You suddenly understand something you've understood all your life, but in a new way. —DORIS LESSING

If I have learned anything in the swift unrolling of the web of time, it is the virtue of tolerance, of moderation in thought and deed, of forbearance toward one's fellowmen. —A.J. CRONIN

Learn as much by writing as by reading. —LORD ACTON

Learning is discovering that something is possible. —FRITZ PERLS

You have learned something. That always feels at first as if you had lost something. —GEORGE BERNARD SHAW

The only things worth learning are the things you learn after you know it all. —HARRY S. TRUMAN

Learning isn't a means to an end; it is an end in itself. —ROBERT A. HEINLEIN

Learning learns but one lesson: doubt!
—George Bernard Shaw

The important thing is not to stop questioning.
—Albert Einstein

Chance favors the prepared mind.
—Louis Pasteur

You cannot teach a man anything. You can only help him to find it within himself.   —Galileo

The real voyage of discovery consists not in seeking new landscapes but in having new eyes.
—Marcel Proust

Know Thyself

What and how much had I lost by trying to do only what was expected of me instead of what I myself had wished to do? What a waste, what a senseless waste.
—Ralph Ellison

Resolve to be thyself and know that he who finds himself loses his misery.   —Matthew Arnold

Any path is only a path, and there is no affront, to one-self or to others, in dropping it if that is what your heart tells you.   —CARLOS CASTANEDA

We only do well the things we like doing.
—COLETTE

Your vision will become clear only when you can look into your own heart. . . . Who looks outside, dreams; who looks inside, awakes.   —CARL JUNG

What a man thinks of himself, that is which deter-mines, or rather indicates, his fate.
—HENRY DAVID THOREAU

If a man does not keep pace with his companions, perhaps it is because he hears a different drummer. Let him step to the music he hears, however measured or far away.   —HENRY DAVID THOREAU

Some people march to a different drummer—and some people polka.   —ANONYMOUS

No one can make you feel inferior without your con-sent.   —ELEANOR ROOSEVELT

To know oneself, one should assert oneself.
—ALBERT CAMUS

Satisfaction will come to those who please themselves.
—ARNOLD LOBEL

I don't have to be what you don't want me to be.
—MUHAMMAD ALI

As soon as you trust yourself, you will know how to live.   —GOETHE

Follow your own bent, no matter what people say.
—KARL MARX

"Know thyself" means this—that you get acquainted with what you know, and what you can do.
—MENANDER OF ATHENS

"Know thyself"—a maxim as pernicious as it is ugly. Whoever studies himself arrests his own development. A caterpillar that set out really to "know itself" would never become a butterfly.   —ANDRE GIDE

No one knows what it is that he can do till he tries.
—PUBLILIUS SYRUS

The duty to be alive is the same as the duty to become oneself, to develop into the individual one potentially is.   —ERICH FROMM

How can you come to know yourself? Never by think-ing, always by doing.   —GOETHE

Learn to like what you are, for you take yourself with you wherever you go.   —K. O'BRIEN

If you find out what it is you love to do and give your whole life to it, then there is no contradiction, and in that state your being is your doing.

—J. KRISHNAMURTI

There is nothing that has to be done—there is only someone to be.   —JACQUELYN SMALL

When we begin to trust ourselves more, the body be-gins to renew itself and becomes healthy and filled with life energy.   —SHAKTI GAWAIN

Get down to your real self . . . and let that speak. One's real self is always vital, and gives the impression of vitality.   —JOHN BURROUGHS

Insist on yourself; never imitate.

—RALPH WALDO EMERSON

What's a man's first duty? The answer is brief: To be himself.   —ANONYMOUS

If a man happens to find himself he has a mansion which he can inhabit with dignity all the days of his life.   —JAMES MICHENER

Miracles don't come from the cold intellect. They come from finding your authentic self and following what you feel is your own true course in life.
                                          —DR. BERNIE SIEGEL

A human being is only interesting if he's in contact with himself. I learned you have to trust yourself, be what you are, and do what you ought to do the way you should do it. You have got to discover you, what you do, and trust it.   —BARBRA STREISAND

People often say that this or that person has not yet found himself. But the self is not something that one finds. It is something one creates.   —THOMAS SZASZ

The growth in self awareness comes from becoming more and more who I am. It is less and less a struggle with myself. And it has less and less to do with anything I do. The only thing I do not have to struggle with is being myself.   —JOHN BRADSHAW

Life Is . . .

Life is rather like a tin of sardines—we're all of us looking for the key.　　　　　　　　　　　—ALAN BENNETT

Life is a tragedy when seen in close-up, but a comedy in long-shot.　　　　　　　　　　—CHARLIE CHAPLIN

Life is just one damned thing after another.
　　　　　　　　　　　　　—ELBERT HUBBARD

Life is like a sewer. What you get out of it depends on what you put into it.　　　　　　　　—TOM LEHRER

Life is what happens to you while you're busy making other plans.　　　　　　　　　　—JOHN LENNON

Life is a fatal adventure. It can only have one end. So why not make it as far-ranging and free as possible?
　　　　　　　　　　　　—ALEXANDER ELIOT

Life is not a trip in itself. It's not a goal. It's a process. You get there step by step. And if every step is wondrous, and every step is magical, that's what life will be. —LEO BUSCAGLIA

Life is really very simple. What we give out, we get back. —LOUISE L. HAY

All life is an experiment.
—OLIVER WENDELL HOLMES, JR.

Life, the biological chain that holds our parts together, is only as strong as the weakest vital link.
—HANS SELYE

Life is short, but it is long enough to ruin any man who wants to be ruined. —JOSH BILLINGS (H.W. SHAW)

Life is easier to take than you'd think; all that is necessary is to accept the impossible, do without the indispensable, and bear the intolerable.
—KATHLEEN NORRIS

Life is like a ten-speed bike. Most of us have gears we never use. —CHARLES SCHULZ

Life is like riding a bicycle. You don't fall off unless you stop pedaling. —CLAUDE PEPPER

Life's a pretty precious and wonderful thing. You can't sit down and let it lap around you . . . you have to plunge into it, you have to dive through it.

—Kyle Crichton

Life is what we are alive to. It is not length but breadth. To be alive only to appetite, pleasure, pride, money-making, and not to goodness, kindness, purity, love, history, poetry, music, flowers, stars, God, and eternal hope is to be all but dead.

—Maltbie D. Babcock

Life is an experience of ripening. The green fruit has but small resemblance to that which is matured.

—Charles B. Newcomb

It has begun to occur to me that life is a stage I'm going through.

—Ellen Goodman

Life is subject to change without notice.

—Richard Eaton

The art of life is the art of avoiding pain.

—Thomas Jefferson

Life is like a game of cards. The hand that is dealt you represents determinism. The way you play it is free will.

—Jawaharlal Nehru

Life is no brief candle to me. It is a sort of splendid torch which I have got hold of for the moment, and I want to make it burn as brightly as possible before handing it on to future generations.
—GEORGE BERNARD SHAW

Life is like music; it must be composed by ear, feeling, and instinct, not by rule.   —SAMUEL BUTLER

Life is like playing a violin solo in public and learning the instrument as one goes on.   —SAMUEL BUTLER

Life is to be lived. If you have to support yourself, you had bloody well better find some way that is going to be interesting. And you don't do that by sitting around wondering about yourself.   —KATHARINE HEPBURN

Life is something like this trumpet. If you don't put anything in it, you don't get anything out.
—W.C. HANDY

Life is really simple, but men insist on making it complicated.   —CONFUCIUS

Life is a full-time job.
—DR. RICHARD DIAMOND

Life is long to the miserable, but short to the happy.
—PUBLILIUS SYRUS

Life is 440 horsepower in a 2-cylinder engine.

—HENRY MILLER

Life is not always what one wants it to be, but to make the best of it as it is, is the only way of being happy.

—JENNIE JEROME CHURCHILL

Life is a great big canvas, and you should throw all the paint on it you can.   —DANNY KAYE

Life is not length but depth.

—ANONYMOUS

Life/Living

I am not going to fight against death but for life.

—NORBERT SEGARD

Life was meant to be lived, and curiosity must be kept alive. One must never, for whatever reason, turn his back on life.   —ELEANOR ROOSEVELT

A man should live only to satisfy his curiosity.

—JEWISH PROVERB

Be not afraid of life. Believe that life is worth living, and your belief will help create the fact.

—WILLIAM JAMES

Life truly lived is a risky business, and if one puts up too many fences against risk one ends by shutting out life itself.   —KENNETH S. DAVIS

As you begin living *your* life, taking risks to do what you really want to do, you will find things fall into place and you "just happen" to be in the right place at the right time. Even elevator doors start to open when you arrive.   —DR. BERNIE SIEGEL

It ain't over till it's over.

—YOGI BERRA

Life can only be understood backwards; but it can only be lived forwards.   —SOREN KIERKEGAARD

We are here to add what we can *to*, not to get what we can *from*, Life.   —WILLIAM OSLER

We make a living by what we get, but we make a life by what we give.   —NORMAN MACEWAN

The aim of life is to live, and to live means to be aware, joyously, drunkenly, serenely, divinely aware.

—HENRY MILLER

What we call the secret of happiness is no more a secret than our willingness to choose life.

—Leo Buscaglia

LIVE, so you do not have to look back and say: "God, how I have wasted my life."

—Elisabeth Kübler-Ross

The real purpose of attaining better physical health and longer life is not just the enjoyment of a pain and disease-free existence, but a higher divine purpose for which life was given to us.   —Paavo Airola

May you live all the days of your life.

—Jonathan Swift

The more passionately we love life, the more intensely we experience the joy of life.   —Jurgen Moltman

I think of life as a good book. The further you get into it, the more it begins to make sense.

—Harold S. Kushner

In three words, I can sum up everything I've learned about life: It goes on.   —Robert Frost

Do not take life too seriously—you will never get out of it alive.   —Elbert Hubbard

We are wide-eyed in contemplating the possibility that life may exist elsewhere in the universe, but we wear blinders in contemplating the possibilities of life on earth.   —Norman Cousins

Don't be afraid your life will end; be afraid that it will never begin.   —Grace Hansen

It is not doing the thing we like to do, but liking the thing we have to do, that makes life blessed.
                    —Goethe

It is not the things we accomplish that are important, it is the very act of living that is truly important.
                    —Dr. Bill Jackson

Let us endeavor so to live that when we come to die even the undertaker will be sorry.   —Mark Twain

In the time of your life, live.
                    —William Saroyan

You don't get to choose how you're going to die, or when. You can only decide how you're going to live. Now.   —Joan Baez

The proper function of man is to live, not to exist.
                    —Jack London

As long as you live, keep learning how to live.
—SENECA

It matters not how long you live, but how well.
—PUBLILIUS SYRUS

Each day should be passed as though it were our last.
—PUBLILIUS SYRUS

To be able to look back upon one's past life with satisfaction is to live twice.   —MARTIAL

While we live, let us live.
—MEDIEVAL LATIN PROVERB

Clothe warm, eat little, drink well, so thou shalt live.
—JOHN FLORIO

In spite of the cost of living, it's still popular.
—KATHLEEN NORRIS

Live all you can; it's a mistake not to. It doesn't so much matter what you do in particular, so long as you have your life. If you haven't had that *what* have you had?   —HENRY JAMES

Living well and beautifully and justly are all one thing.
—SOCRATES

We are always getting ready to live, but never living.
—RALPH WALDO EMERSON

Dying is no accomplishment; we all do that. Living is the thing.   —RED SMITH

So live that you wouldn't be ashamed to sell the family parrot to the town gossip.   —WILL ROGERS

There's Tarzan captured in the land of the Fire Queen and ready to be sacrificed. He's tied up hand and foot and being carried up to the sacrificial altar. He's surrounded by 5000 of these fierce beastlike characters and a knife is about to be plunged into his heart and somebody says to him, "My God, Tarzan, why are you smiling?" And Tarzan says, "Because I'm still alive."
—DICK YORK, PARAPHRASING
EDGAR RICE BURROUGHS.

Try as much as possible to be wholly alive, with all your might, and when you laugh, laugh like hell and when you get angry, get good and angry. Try to be alive. You will be dead soon enough.
—WILLIAM SAROYAN

If you think nobody cares if you're alive, try missing a couple of car payments.   —EARL WILSON

Longevity

The ingredients of health and long life are great temperance, open air, easy labor, and little care.
—Philip Sidney

To lengthen thy Life, lessen thy meals.
—Benjamin Franklin

A cool mouth and warm feet live long.
—George Herbert

You could say people are living longer because of the decline in religion. Not many people believe in the hereafter, so they keep going.   —Dr. Cyril Clarke

Always do one thing less than you think you can do.
—Bernard Baruch, when asked his secret of longevity

He had decided to live forever or die in the attempt.
—Joseph Heller

LONGEVITY, n. Uncommon extension of the fear of death.
—Ambrose Bierce

The brain is the organ of longevity.

—George Alban Sacher

My wife likes to chew a clove of garlic. She thinks it will help her outlive me so she can dye her hair blue and go to Florida and spend my insurance money running around with a gigolo.   —Mike Royko

I attribute my long life to inward calm.

—An old Chinese man before his death

If you exercise regularly, you'll gain four years of future. If you don't smoke, you'll gain from three to eight years. If you're moderate in your drinking, you'll gain one year. If you practice weight control, you'll add between two and eight years, depending on how many pounds you aren't overweight. And if you'll simply take time every year for a preventive medical checkup, you'll add two more years to your future. That's a minimum of twelve years and a possible twenty-three years added to your life.

—Dr. Kenneth H. Cooper

The secret of prolonging life consists in not shortening it.   —E.V. Feuchtersleben

> Get up at five, have lunch at nine,
> Supper at five, retire at nine.
> And you will live to ninety-nine.
>
> —Rabelais

Aging seems to be the only available way to live a long
time.   —DANIEL-FRANCOIS-ESPRIT AUBER

People always wonder how I have achieved such a ripe
age, and I can only say I never felt the urge to partake
of the grape, the grain, or the weed, but I do eat everything.   —MARY BORAH, AT THE AGE OF 100

Despair of all recovery spoils longevity,
And makes men's miseries of alarming brevity.
                              —LORD BYRON

Do not try to live forever. You will not succeed.
                         —GEORGE BERNARD SHAW

They live ill who expect to live always.
                              —PUBLILIUS SYRUS

Keep breathing.

                              —SOPHIE TUCKER

Love

Love cures people—both the ones who give it and the
ones who receive it.   —KARL A. MENNINGER

Love is a medicine for the sickness of the world; a prescription often given, too rarely taken.

—Karl A. Menninger

We like someone *because*. We love someone *although*.

—Henri de Montherlant

True love never grows old.

—Old Proverb

Love is, above all, the gift of oneself.

—Jean Anouilh

Just a little more loving and a lot less fighting and the world would be all right.   —Mae West

Work and love—these are the basics. Without them there is neurosis.   —Theodore Reik

Infantile love follows the principle: "I love because I am loved." Mature love follows the principle: "I am loved because I love." Immature love says: "I love you because I need you." Mature love says: "I need you because I love you."   —Erich Fromm

Love is when each person is more concerned for the other than for one's self.   —David Frost

Love is the triumph of imagination over intelliegence.
—H.L. Mencken

If you would be loved, love and be lovable.
—Benjamin Franklin

If love does not know how to give and take without restrictions, it is not love, but a transaction.
—Emma Goldman

To love is to place our happiness in the happiness of another.
—Leibnitz

You give but little when you give of your possessions. It is when you give of yourself that you truly give.
—Kahlil Gibran

Love is letting go of fear.
—Gerald Jampolsky

Healing is knowing that the only reality in the universe is love, and that love is the most important healer known to the world.
—Gerald Jampolsky

Love is life in all its aspects. And if you miss love, you miss life.
—Leo Buscaglia

There is nothing greater in life than loving another and being loved in return, for loving is the ultimate of experiences.   —LEO BUSCAGLIA

I will love you no matter what. I will love you if you are stupid, if you slip and fall on your face, if you do the wrong thing, if you make mistakes, if you behave like a human being—I will love you no matter.
                                    —LEO BUSCAGLIA

There is no difficulty that enough love will not conquer; no disease that enough love will not heal; no door that enough love will not open. . . . It makes no difference how deeply seated may be the trouble; how hopeless the outlook; how muddled the tangle; how great the mistake. A sufficient realization of love will dissolve it all. If only you could love enough you would be the happiest and most powerful being in the world.   —EMMET FOX

When a man has a philosophy that includes love, it also includes philanthropy, it includes understanding, sharing, peace, and harmony—and he is able to put all these things together—then that man is going to give his body the best care possible.   —BERNARD JENSEN

Love doesn't just sit there, like a stone; it has to be made, like bread; remade all the time, made new.
                                    —URSULA K. LE GUIN

There is no love sincerer than the love of food.
—GEORGE BERNARD SHAW

Age does not protect you from love. But love, to some extent, protects you from age.   —JEANNE MOREAU

If you judge people, you have no time to love them.
—MOTHER TERESA

Love is all we have, the only way that each can help the other.   —EURIPIDES

Power said to the world, "You are mine." The world kept it prisoner on her throne. Love said to the world, "I am thine." The world gave it the freedom of her house.   —RABINDRANATH TAGORE

The day will come when, after harnessing the winds, the tides, and gravitation, we shall harness for God the energies of love. And on that day, for the second time in the history of the world, man will have discovered fire.   —TEILHARD DE CHARDIN

We all have our own individual way of expressing love, and when we discover what it is, then we will live the longest, be the healthiest, and enjoy life the most, as well as become able to receive the most love from others.   —DR. BERNIE SIEGEL

Healing is accomplished through love and *is* love. And love is the uniting principle in all healing approaches.
—HUGH PRATHER

The more I can love everything—the trees, the land, the water, my fellow men, women, and children, and myself—the more health I am going to experience and the more of my real self I am going to be.
—O. CARL SIMONTON

Love is a great thing, a good above all others, which alone maketh every burden light.
—THOMAS À KEMPIS

True love heals and affects spiritual growth.
—JOHN BRADSHAW

Rub your eyes and purify your heart and prize above all else in the world those who love you and who wish you well.
—ALEXANDER SOLZHENITSYN

Love, to me, means being considerate of others, having compassion for others, being fair to others. Love is *not* expecting things from others. Love is being aware of others. Love is giving as much of yourself as you can, plus a little extra.
—JOSEPH RAYMOND

Love thy neighbor as thyself, but choose your neighborhood.
—LOUISE BEAL

If lots more of us loved each other, we'd solve lots more problems. And then the world would be a *gasser*.
—LOUIS ARMSTRONG

Man must evolve for all human conflict a method which rejects revenge, aggression and retaliation. The foundation of such a method is love.
—MARTIN LUTHER KING, JR.

Love is an excess of friendship.
—ARISTOTLE

There is no surprise more magical than the surprise of being loved. It is God's finger on man's shoulder.
—CHARLES MORGAN

In the final analysis, we must love in order not to fall ill.
—SIGMUND FREUD

Love is the most powerful healing force there is. Love stimulates the immune system. We cannot heal or become whole in an atmosphere of hatred. Love moves us from being a victim to becoming a winner.
—LOUISE L. HAY

Measure/Worth

Health is no other (as the learned hold)
But a just measure both of heat and cold.
—ROBERT HERRICK

Measure your health by your sympathy with morning and spring. If there is no response in you to the awakening of nature, if the prospect of an early morning walk does not banish sleep, if the warble of the first bluebird does not thrill you, know that the morning and spring of your life are past. Thus may you feel your pulse.
—HENRY DAVID THOREAU

The measure of a man's life is the well spending of it, and not the length.
—PLUTARCH

The ultimate measure of a man is not where he stands in moments of comfort, but where he stands at times of challenge and controversy.
—MARTIN LUTHER KING, JR.

The true test of a man's worth is not his theology but his life.   —THE TALMUD

It is not what he has, nor even what he does, which directly expresses the worth of man, but what he is.
                                          —HENRI F. AMIEL

A real man's worth is determined by what he does when he has nothing to do.   —MEGIDDO MESSAGE

Every man is worth just so much as the things are worth about which he busies himself.
                                          —MARCUS AURELIUS

Nothing is worth more than this day.
                                          —GOETHE

For anything worth having one must pay the price; and the price is always work, patience, love, self-sacrifice.
                                          —JOHN BURROUGHS

What is the worth of anything
But for the happiness 'twill bring?
                                          —RICHARD CAMBRIDGE

We can secure other people's approval if we do right and try hard, but our own is worth a hundred of it.
                                          —MARK TWAIN

Health is worth more than learning.

—THOMAS JEFFERSON

Try not to become a man of success but rather try to become a man of value. —ALBERT EINSTEIN

He who undervalues himself is justly undervalued by others. —WILLIAM HAZLITT

Medicine

There's no fun in medicine, but there's a lot of medicine in fun. —ANONYMOUS

He who lives medically lives miserably.

—ROBERT BURTON

A cheerful heart is good medicine, but a crushed spirit dries up the bones. —BIBLE, PROVERBS

It is the sick who need medicine and not the well.

—THOMAS JEFFERSON

Health is the state about which medicine has nothing to say. —W.H. AUDEN

We have not lost faith, but we have transferred it from God to the medical profession.

—GEORGE BERNARD SHAW

Formerly, when religion was strong and science weak, men mistook magic for medicine; now, when science is strong and religion weak, men mistake medicine for magic.

—THOMAS SZASZ

In medicine, as in statecraft and propaganda, words are sometimes the most powerful drugs we can use.

—DR. SARA MURRAY JORDAN

The overriding issue before medicine today is one not of proficiency but of humanity.   —NORMAN COUSINS

Throw physic to the dogs; I'll none of it.

—SHAKESPEARE

Nearly all men die of their medicines, not of their diseases.

—MOLIÈRE

Medicine is the only profession that labors incessantly to destroy the reason for its own existence.

—JAMES BRYCE

A temperate diet was all her medicine,
And exercise, and heart's content.

—GEOFFREY CHAUCER

Kitchen physic is the best physic.

—JONATHAN SWIFT

Walking is man's best medicine.

—HIPPOCRATES

A man's own observation, what he finds good of and what he finds hurt of, is the best physic to preserve health. —FRANCIS BACON

Physic, for the most part, is nothing else but the substitute of exercise or temperance. —JOSEPH ADDISON

Medicine is like a woman who changes with the fashions. —AUGUST BIER

After twenty years one is no longer quoted in the medical literature. Every twenty years one sees a republication of the same ideas. —BÉLA SCHICK

Because all the sick do not recover, therefore medicine is no art. —CICERO

Medicine is a collection of uncertain prescriptions, the results of which, taken collectively, are more fatal than useful to mankind. Water, air, and cleanliness are the chief articles in my pharmacopeia.

—NAPOLEON BONAPARTE

Despite all our toil and progress, the art of medicine still falls somewhere between trout casting and spook writing.   —BEN HECHT

The art of medicine is generally a question of time.
                                                     —OVID

I've already had medical attention—a dog licked me when I was on the ground.   —NEIL SIMON

Medicine's art lay in a skillful manipulation of the relationship between doctor and patient which, when combined with the logical use of medicine's science, lead to the best of patient care.
                                      —DR. TRUMAN SCHNABEL

Many medicines, few cures.
                                      —BENJAMIN FRANKLIN

Medicine heals doubts as well as diseases.
                                             —KARL MARX

The prime goal [of medicine] is to alleviate suffering, and not to prolong life.   —CHRISTIAN BARNARD

Nature heals, under the auspices of the medical profession.   —HAVEN EMERSON

The patient's bed is his best medicine.

—ITALIAN PROVERB

Meditation

Don't you know that four-fifths of all our troubles in this life would disappear if we would just sit down and keep still? —CALVIN COOLIDGE

Many techniques and therapies are useful, but nothing is as effective as daily meditation practice to deepen the well from which the thirst for healing may be slaked. —STEPHEN LEVINE

It is only through quieting the mind and senses, and learning to direct the consciousness *inward*, that Self, one's true nature, can be experienced. In this experience peace, knowledge, and bliss become realities. —RICHARD HITTLEMAN

A good program of meditation is, in many ways, quite similar to a good program of physical exercise. Both require repeated hard work. —LAWRENCE LE SHAN

Meditation is not a means to an end. It is both the means and the end. —J. KRISHNAMURTI

Sitting quietly by oneself and being aware of all that's taking place in the mind and body can lead to rejuvenation.   —STAN LIPKIN

I believe meditation is a wonderful way to relax, get in touch with what it is we need to know, and to energize ourselves. Give yourself a few minutes every day to sit in quiet meditation. . . . observe your breathing and allow the thoughts to pass gently through your mind.   —LOUISE L. HAY

Meditation in any of its forms is a wonderful way to quiet the mind and allow your own "knowingness" to come to the surface. I usually just sit with my eyes closed and say, "What is it I need to know?" and then wait quietly for an answer. If the answer comes, fine; if it doesn't, fine. It will come another day.
                                                      —LOUISE L. HAY

Many of us are used to being at the beck and call of the world; meditation is one time you are not. *You must make time for yourself.* If you fail to make time for yourself, always putting other things first, you will never be happy, nor will you make others happy. This is your time. Time you take for yourself to more fully understand the interaction of your mind, body, and spirit.   —JOAN BORYSENKO

Sit still for 15 minutes every day; listen to your breathing; feel it and yourself; and try to think of nothing.
                                                      —ERICH FROMM

In those few moments [of meditation] when the mind becomes calm, we experience a peacefulness, a contentment that is the inner Self, the part of our consciousness that is not conditioned by past experience.
—JOAN BORYSENKO

If we can only set aside a short time every day, quite alone and in as quiet a place as possible, free from interruption, and merely sit or lie quietly, either keeping the mind a blank or calmly thinking of one's work in life, it will be found after a time that we get great help at such moments and, as it were, flashes of knowledge and guidance are given to us. We find that the questions of the difficult problems of life are unmistakably answered, and we become able to choose with confidence the right course.   —DR. EDWARD BACH

Inner silence reduces anxiety, tension, irritability, chronic fatigue, and depression. The positive feelings that accompany such reductions add noticeably to personality development. Self-esteem grows, sociability develops, and doubts and insecurities fade.
—HAROLD BLOOMFIELD

In the West, where the meditative tradition is not strong and people are not in the habit of stopping periodically to become quiet and reevaluate their lives, illness stops a person so he can step back and have an opportunity to take stock of what is important to him.
—MARTIN L. ROSSMAN, M.D.

There was a time not too long ago when a physician who prescribed meditation was regarded as somewhat fringe. Today a good share of physicians are meditating themselves. —ART ULENE, M.D.

Mind

Health is not a condition of matter, but of Mind.
—MARY BAKER EDDY

Drugs, cataplasms and whiskey are stupid substitutes for the dignity and potency of divine Mind, and its efficacy to heal. —MARY BAKER EDDY

Happiness, or misery, is in the mind. It is the mind that lives. —WILLIAM COBBETT

The mind is its own place, and in itself
Can make a heaven of Hell, a hell of Heaven.
—JOHN MILTON

Rule your mind or it will rule you.
—HORACE

Mind moves matter.

—VIRGIL

Much bending breaks the bow; much unbending the mind. —FRANCIS BACON

Medicine has been blind in thinking that matter is more powerful than mind. —DEEPAK CHOPRA

The mind has great influence over the body, and maladies often have their origin there. —MOLIÈRE

The human mind can discipline the body, can set goals for itself, can somehow comprehend its own potentiality and move resolutely forward.

—NORMAN COUSINS

I am finding that nothing can hurt me except my own thoughts, my own mind. —GERALD JAMPOLSKY

Iron rusts from disuse, water loses its purity from stagnation . . . even so does inaction sap the vigors of the mind. —LEONARDO DA VINCI

A mind is healthy when it has no conflict at all; then it can function without any friction and such a mind is a sane, clear mind. —J. KRISHNAMURTI

Mind and Body

A sound mind in a manly body.
>—HOMER, WHEN ASKED THE GREATEST BLESSING
>OF MAN

A strong body makes the mind strong.
>—THOMAS JEFFERSON

All sorts of bodily diseases are produced by half-used minds.   —GEORGE BERNARD SHAW

One of my problems is that I internalize everything. I can't express anger; I grow a tumor instead.
>—WOODY ALLEN

A cancer is not only a physical disease, it is a state of mind.   —DR. MICHAEL M. BADEN

Minds, like bodies, will often fall into a pimpled, ill-conditioned state from mere excess of comfort.
>—CHARLES DICKENS

Fat bodies, lean brains.
>—FRANCIS BEAUMONT
>—JOHN FLETCHER

If you want to know if your brain is flabby, feel of your legs.   —BRUCE BARTON

When the head is a fool, the body is in trouble.
                                         —JEWISH PROVERB

The body is at its best between the ages of thirty and thirty-five; the mind is at its best about the age of forty-nine.   —ARISTOTLE

Reading is to the mind what exercise is to the body.
                                         —RICHARD STEELE

It seems that there is a direct connection between creative thought and involvement in life and the production of epinephrine by the adrenal gland. When the challenge stops, the supply is turned off; the will to live atrophies.   —NORMAN COUSINS

If you are ruled by mind you are a king; if by body, a slave.   —CATO

The most uninformed mind with a healthy body is happier than the wisest valetudinarian.
                                         —THOMAS JEFFERSON

Sickly body, sickly mind.
                                         —GERMAN PROVERB

A sedentary body makes for a sedentary mind.
—Bruce W. Tuckman

The fact that the mind rules the body is, in spite of its neglect by biology and medicine, the most fundamental fact which we know about the process of life.
—Franz Alexander, M.D.

Some element in the mind of the patient makes an important difference in the body's reaction to illness, something as ephemeral as an attitude or feeling that could leave its mark on the body.
—Dr. Steven Locke
—Douglas Colligan

Some say, "The body is in the mind."
Some, "The mind is in the body."
Perhaps we are but body/mind
(a concept that's been ill-defined).
It seems we need to coin a word,
one that won't sound too absurd.
Should this word be "mody?"
Or, should it be "bind?"
The answer, you can see, is hard to find.
(I guess we're in a "mody bind.")
—Dr. Steven Locke

It is not possible to heal the body without engaging the mind's support.
—Meir Schneider

To heal the body without including the mind, without allowing the body/mind to sink into the heart, is to continue the grief of a lifetime.   —STEPHEN LEVINE

The only reason to have a physically strong body is to be able to express our potential that is mental.
—DEAN BLACK

The mind may undoubtedly affect the body; but the body also affects the mind. There is a reaction between them; and by lessening it on either side, you diminish the pain on both.   —LEIGH HUNT

Moderation/Temperance

Wouldst thou be happy, be thou moderate.
—CODE OF MANU, C. 1000 B.C.

Out of moderation, a pure happiness springs.
—GOETHE

Moderation is medicine.
—WILLIAM LANGLAND

In order to be healthy and not to hurt yourself, you must be moderate in eating, sleeping, exercise, play, work, *and* sex! When you indulge in anything to excess, you pay with a deterioration in your health.

—MARILYN DIAMOND

Moderation lasts.

—SENECA

One swears by wholemeal bread, one by sour milk; vegetarianism is the only road to salvation for some, others insist not only on vegetables alone, but on eating those raw. At one time the only thing that matters is calories; at another time they are crazy about vitamins or about roughage. The scientific truth may be put quite briefly; eat moderately, having an ordinary mixed diet, and don't worry.

—ROBERT HUTCHINSON

Temperance is simply a disposition of the mind which sets bounds to the passions.   —THOMAS AQUINAS

Temperance is the noblest gift of the gods.

—EURIPIDES

Is not temperance a virtue? Aye, assuredly it is. But wherefore? Because by restraining enjoyment for a time, it afterwards elevates it to that very pitch which leaves, on the whole, the largest addition to the stock of happiness.   —JEREMY BENTHAM

Temperance has those advantages over all other means of health that it may be practiced by all ranks and conditions, at any season, or in any place. It is a kind of regimen into which every man may put himself, without interruption to business, expense of money, or loss of time. —JOSEPH ADDISON

Temperance is the greatest of all virtues.

—PLUTARCH

Temperance is the best physic.

—ENGLISH PROVERB

Temperate in all things.

—BIBLE, CORINTHIANS

Do not charge, most innocent nature,
As if she would her children should be riotous
With her abundance; she, good cateress,
Means her provision only to the good,
That live according to her sober laws,
And holy dictate of spare temperance.

—JOHN MILTON

Be sober and temperate, and you will be healthy.

—BENJAMIN FRANKLIN

Enough is as good as a feast.

—JOHN HEYWOOD

The frugal eater is probably the wisest person . . . and temperance is probably the greatest Key of all. Temperate people have a philosophy that is good for their bodies—that does not tear them to pieces—and that allows them to repair and rebuild beautifully in their natural environment.   —BERNARD JENSEN

He that knoweth when he hath enough is no fool.
                              —JOHN HEYWOOD

Enough is abundance to the wise.
                                    —EURIPIDES

Enough is better than too much.
                               —FRENCH PROVERB

'Tis not so deep as a well, nor so wide as a church door; but 'tis enough, 'twill serve.   —SHAKESPEARE

Eat not to dullness; drink not to elevation.
                              —BENJAMIN FRANKLIN

Indulge the body only so far as is needful for health.
                                       —SENECA

Be it thy use to keep these things in check, the belly first, then sleep, desire and anger.   —PYTHAGORAS

It is necessary to subject appetite to reason.

—CICERO

I always get up from the table a little hungry.

—DR. NATHANIEL EMMONS

He knows to live who keeps the middle state.

—ALEXANDER POPE

When it comes to your health, I recommend frequent doses of that rare commodity among Americans—common sense.   —DR. VINCENT ASKEY

> Tho' deep yet clear, tho' gentle yet
>   not dull;
> Strong without rage, without o'erflowing
>   full.

—JOHN DENHAM

Moment to Moment/The Present

If we live in the moment, use the moment to the full, we will never be bored and seldom depressed.

—KAREN CASEY
—MARTHA VANCEBURG

To live exhilaratingly in and for the moment is deadly serious work, fun of the most exhausting sort.

—BARBARA GRIZZUTI HARRISON

Life is a succession of moments,
To live each one is to succeed.

—CORITA KENT

the thing about livin'
is it not true?
is that each moment
is entirely new.

—GERRY DOUD

To be concentrated means to live fully in the present, in the here and now, and not to think of the next thing to be done, while I am doing something right now.

—ERICH FROMM

In any weather, at any hour of the day or night, I have been anxious to improve the nick of time, and notch it on my stick too; to stand on the meeting of two eternities, the past and future, which is precisely the present moment; to toe that line.

—HENRY DAVID THOREAU

Life is a great, wondrous mystery, and the only thing we know that we have for sure is what is right here right now. Don't miss it. To use it all up is love.

—LEO BUSCAGLIA

You must live in the present, launch yourself on every wave, find your eternity in each moment. Fools stand on their island opportunities and look toward another land. There is no other land; there is no other life but this, or the like of this.   —HENRY DAVID THOREAU

Now or never.

—ARISTOPHANES

Let's have a merry journey, and shout about how light is good and dark is not. What we should do is not future ourselves so much. We should *now* ourselves more. "*Now* thyself" is more important than "Know thyself." Reason is what tells us to ignore the present and live in the future. So all we do is make plans. We think that somewhere there are going to be green pastures. It's crazy. Heaven is nothing but a grand, monumental instance of future. Listen, *now* is good. *Now* is wonderful.   —MEL BROOKS

The past is over and done and cannot be changed. This is the only moment we can experience. Even when we grudge about the past, we are experiencing our memory of it in this moment, and losing the real experience of this moment in the process.

—LOUISE L. HAY

When we live in the past or focus too much on the future, we rob ourselves of the now!

—ELLEN KREIDMAN

If I had only . . .
forgotten future greatness
and looked at the green things and the buildings
and reached out to those around me
and smelled the air
and ignored the forms and the self-styled obligations
and heard the rain on the roof
and put my arms around my wife
. . . and it's not too late

—HUGH PRATHER

There is no time like the present time.

—TOBIAS SMOLLETT

The present hour alone is man's.

—SAMUEL JOHNSON

Seize the day.

—HORACE

One must learn to be concentrated in everything one does, in listening to music, in reading a book, in talking to a person, in seeing a view. The activity at this very moment must be the only thing that matters, to which one is fully given. —ERICH FROMM

Money

The poorest man would not part with health for money, but the richest would gladly part with all his money for health. —C.C. COLTON

Money-giving is a very good criterion of a person's mental health. Generous people are rarely mentally ill people. —KARL A. MENNINGER

Health and money go far.
—GEORGE HERBERT

Money may be the husk of many things, but not the kernel. It brings you food, but not appetite; medicine, but not health; acquaintances, but not friends; servants, but not loyalty; days of joy, but not peace or happiness. —HENRIK IBSEN

Money is like an arm or a leg—use it or lose it.
—HENRY FORD

It's good to have money and the things that money can buy, but it's good, too, to check up once in a while to make sure you haven't lost the things money can't buy.
—GEORGE HORACE LORIMER

Superfluous wealth can buy superfluities only. Money is not required to buy one necessary of the soul.
— HENRY DAVID THOREAU

The darkest hour in any man's life is when he sits down to plan how to get money without earning it.
— HORACE GREELEY

The lack of money is the root of all evil.
— MARK TWAIN

Money is like manure. If you spread it around it does a lot of good, but if you pile it up in one place it stinks like hell.
— CLINT MURCHISON

Make all you can, save all you can, give all you can.
— JOHN WESLEY

If ever you have a lump of money large enough to be of any use, and can spare it, don't give it away: find some needed job that nobody is doing and get it done.
— GEORGE BERNARD SHAW

Morality of Health

To preserve health is a moral and religious duty, for health is the basis of all social virtues.

—SAMUEL JOHNSON

Health is, indeed, so necessary to all the duties as well as pleasures of life, that the crime of squandering it is equal to the folly; and he that for a short gratification brings weakness and diseases upon himself, and for the pleasure of a few years passed in the tumults of diversion and clamors of merriment, condemns the maturer and more experienced part of his life to the chamber and the couch, may be justly reproached, not only as a spendthrift of his happiness, but as a robber of the public; as a wretch that has voluntarily disqualified himself for the business of his station, and refused that part which Providence assigns him in the general task of human nature.   —SAMUEL JOHNSON

Take care of your health; you have no right to neglect it, and thus become a burden to yourself, and perhaps to others.   —WILLIAM HALL

It's your responsibility to stay healthy, not only to make it easier on yourself, but to make it easier on others.   —JERRY LIPKIN

The preservation of health is a duty. Few seem conscious that there is such a thing as physical morality.
—HERBERT SPENCER

Failure due to abdication of responsibility is everywhere: obesity, alcoholism, drug addiction, mental crack-ups, crippled hearts, sports injuries and millions in chronic pain. We can look everywhere for someone else to blame, but in the end we must look to ourselves. Then we must change.   —BONNIE PRUDDEN

You are responsible for your own life and have a job to perform in your health care.   —NEIL A. FIORE

At any age, a person has the pulse he or she deserves. I regard my heart rate as my own responsibility.
—DR. GEORGE SHEEHAN

Health is the first requisite after morality.
—THOMAS JEFFERSON

What is moral is what you feel good after, and what is immoral is what you feel bad after.
—ERNEST HEMINGWAY

Indigestion is charged by God with enforcing morality on the stomach.   —VICTOR HUGO

Past, Present, Future

Look not mournfully into the Past. It comes not back again. Wisely improve the Present. It is thine. Go forth to meet the shadowy Future, without fear, and with a manly heart.　　　　—HENRY WADSWORTH LONGFELLOW

> Trust no future, howe'er pleasant;
> Let the dead past bury its dead;
> Act—act in the living present,
> Heart within, the God o'erhead.
> 　　　　—HENRY WADSWORTH LONGFELLOW

> We can learn from the Past;
> But it's the Present, that's the thing;
> The Future is just beginning.
> 　　　　—JOSEPH RAYMOND

Live neither in the past nor in the future, but let each day's work absorb your entire energies, and satisfy your widest ambition.　　　　—WILLIAM OSLER

The only way to ensure a good future is to maximize the present. Focus on the present. Make the present good!   —MARILYN DIAMOND

Some there are that torment themselves afresh with the memory of what is past; others, again, afflict themselves with the apprehension of evils to come; and very ridiculously—for the one does not now concern us, and the other not yet. . . . One should count each day a separate life.   —SENECA

The past was nothing to her; offered no lesson which she was willing to heed. The future was a mystery which she never attempted to penetrate. The present alone was significant.   —KATE CHOPIN

Live and make the present hour pleasant and cheerful. Keep your mind out of the past, and keep it out of the future.   —JOHN A SCHINDLER

Even God cannot change the past.

                                            —AGATHON

Shut out all of your past except that which will help you weather your tomorrows.   —WILLIAM OSLER

Redeem thy mis-spent time that's past;
Live this day, as if 'twere thy last.
                                        —THOMAS KEN

The error of the past is the success of the future. A mistake is evidence that someone tried to do something.
—ANONYMOUS

Most of us spend 59 minutes in an hour living in the past with regret for lost joys, or shame for things badly done . . . or in a future which we either long for or dread.   —STORM JAMESON

The present time has one advantage over every other. It is our own.   —C.C. COLTON

The contemporary time is always the best time to live. It is a mistake to say the best age is one without problems.   —DANIEL J. BOORSTIN

Never make forecasts, especially about the future.
—SAMUEL GOLDWYN

My interest is in the future because I am going to spend the rest of my life there.   —CHARLES F. KETTERING

Every thought we think, every word we speak, is creating the future.   —LOUISE L. HAY

The best thing about the future is that it comes only one day at a time.   —ABRAHAM LINCOLN

The mind that is anxious about the future is miserable.

—SENECA

The future is purchased by the present.

—SAMUEL JOHNSON

Patience

Dear God—I pray for patience. And I want it *right now*!

—OREN ARNOLD

Patience is the best remedy that is for a sick man, the most precious plaster that is for any wound.

—JOHN FLORIO

Patience is a particular requirement. Without it you can destroy in an hour what it might take you weeks to repair.

—CHARLIE W. SHEDD

Patience is the key to Paradise.

—TURKISH PROVERB

A handful of patience is worth more than a bushel of brains.

—DUTCH PROVERB

Never think that God's delays are God's denials. Hold on; hold fast; hold out. Patience is genius.
— COMTE DE BUFFON

To have an idea of what patience is one need only watch a child learning to walk. — ERICH FROMM

Patience is bitter, but its fruit sweet.
— JEAN JACQUES ROUSSEAU

He who has patience goes soundly and a long way.
— ITALIAN PROVERB

The creating of anything worthwhile takes patience and energy. — ANONYMOUS

Patience and fortitude conquer all things.
— RALPH WALDO EMERSON

Be patient with everyone, but above all with yourself.
— SAINT FRANCIS DE SALES

Be patient with the faults of others; they have to be patient with yours. — OUR DAILY BREAD

Patience is a virtue that carries a lot of WAIT!
— OUR DAILY BREAD

How poor are they who have not patience. What wound did ever heal but by degrees?   —SHAKESPEARE

He that can have patience can have what he will.
—BENJAMIN FRANKLIN

If God has taken away all means of seeking remedy, there is nothing left but patience.   —JOHN LOCKE

All men commend patience, although few be willing to practice it.   —THOMAS À KEMPIS

> Never a tear bedims the eye
> That time and patience will not dry.
> —BRET HARTE

Patience is the companion of wisdom.
—SAINT AUGUSTINE

Patience is a gift that God gives only to those He loves.
—MOROCCAN PROVERB

Peace and Harmony

For peace of mind, resign as general manager of the universe. —LARRY EISENBERG

The peaceful are the strong.
—OLIVER WENDELL HOLMES, SR.

If it be possible, as much as lieth in you, live peaceably with all men. —BIBLE, ROMANS

First keep thyself in peace and then thou shalt be able to pacify others. A peaceable man doth more good than he that is well learned. —THOMAS À KEMPIS

We would have much peace if we would not busy ourselves with the sayings and doings of others.
—THOMAS À KEMPIS

Nothing can bring you peace but yourself.
—RALPH WALDO EMERSON

Without peace of mind, life is just a shadow of its possibilities. —JOAN BORYSENKO

Without inner peace, it is impossible to have world peace.   —14TH DALAI LAMA

If I can find peace within myself, then I'm much more apt to influence peace outside of myself.
                                    —DR. RICHARD DIAMOND

I think that world healing begins with the individual. I don't think you can go out into the world and heal, on an effective level, if you don't start at home first, with yourself, with the people around you.
                                    —LYNN ANDREWS

As is the human body, so is the cosmic body.
As is the human mind, so is the cosmic mind.
As is the microcosm, so is the macrocosm.
As is the atom, so is the universe.
                                    —AYURVEDA SAYING

If there is righteousness in the heart, there will be
    beauty in the character.
If there is beauty in the character, there will be
    harmony in the home.
If there is harmony in the home, there will be
    order in the nation.
When there is order in the nation, there will be
    peace in the world.
                                    —CHINESE SAYING

We cannot separate the healing of the individual from the healing of the planet. They are one and the same, because the consciousness of each individual is connected to the collective consciousness. Although we are individuals, we are also each a part of the whole. As we begin to heal ourselves as individuals, we also naturally shift the consciousness of the entire planet. And as the collective consciousness begins to shift, we are each in turn affected by it. Thus, the more people change their consciousness and their way of life, the more the world changes; and the more the world changes, the more individuals change.

—SHAKTI GAWAIN

But where was I to start? The world is so vast, I shall start with the country I know best, my own. But my country is so very large. I had better start with my town. But my town, too, is large. I had best start with my street.. No, my home. No, my family. Never mind, I shall start with myself. —ELIE WIESEL

Think globally, act locally.

—BUMPER STICKER, 1980s

Smiling is very important. If we are not able to smile, then the world will not have peace . . . .It is with our capacity of smiling, breathing and being peace that we can make peace. —THKH NHAT HANH

If we are not in harmony with ourselves, how can we possibly be in harmony with anyone else, much less the world we inhabit?   —SHIRLEY MACLAINE

The fewer the desires, the more peace.
                                        —THOMAS WILSON

Undisturbed calmness of mind is attained by cultivating friendliness toward the happy, compassion for the unhappy, delight in the virtuous, and indifference toward the wicked.   —PATANJALI

Avoid friends and followers who are detrimental to thy peace of mind and spiritual growth.
                        —TIBETAN ROSARY OF PRECIOUS GEMS

Those who are at war with others are not at peace with themselves.   —WILLIAM HAZLITT

Do not lose your inward peace for anything whatsoever, even if your whole world seems upset.
                                —SAINT FRANCIS DE SALES

To get peace, if you want it, make for yourselves nests of pleasant thoughts.   —JOHN RUSKIN

There is no way to peace. Peace is the way.
                                        —A.J. MUSTE

We must steadfastly practice peace, imagining our minds as a lake ever to be kept calm, without waves, or even ripples, to disturb its tranquility, and gradually develop this state of peace until no event of life, no circumstance, no other personality is able under any condition to ruffle the surface of that lake or raise within us any feelings of irritability, depression or doubt. . . . and though at first it may seem to be beyond our dreams, it is in reality, with patience and perseverance, within the reach of us all.   —DR. EDWARD BACH

The first step toward making the world a better place to live must be to improve the health of everyone. The only way to rid humanity of disease is for each person to become healthy, to become his or her own healer. Freed of preoccupation with painful or ailing bodies, we can concentrate our attention on deepening our awareness. From the base of individuals learning to care for their health, we can create a new world. We need to free the mind so that it will not inhibit the body from realizing its true potential.

—MEIR SCHNEIDER

Perseverance

Perseverance is not a long race; it is many short races one after another.   —WALTER ELLIOTT

Press on: Nothing in the world can take the place of perseverance. Talent will not; nothing is more common than unsuccessful men with talent. Genius will not; unrewarded genius is almost a proverb. Education will not; the world is full of educated derelicts. Persistence and determination alone are omnipotent.

—CALVIN COOLIDGE

Great works are performed not by strength, but perseverance.   —SAMUEL JOHNSON

Keep on going and the chances are you will stumble on something, perhaps when you are least expecting it. I have never heard of anyone stumbling on something sitting down.   —CHARLES F. KETTERING

Never give up and never give in.

—HUBERT H. HUMPHREY

Never say die.

—CHARLES DICKENS

Tough times never last; tough people always do.

—GEORGE KREVSKY

Let me tell you the secret that has led me to my goal. My strength lies solely in my tenacity.

—LOUIS PASTEUR

Fall seven times, stand up eight.

—JAPANESE PROVERB

Consider the postage stamp: its usefulness consists in the ability to stick to one thing till it gets there.

—JOSH BILLINGS (H.W. SHAW)

Endure and persist; this pain will turn to your good.

—OVID

Enjoy when you can, and endure when you must.

—GOETHE

To struggle when hope is banished.
To live when life's salt is gone!
To dwell in a dream that's vanished—
To endure, and go calmly on!

—BEN JONSON

His [Ulysses'] secret is that he endures. He accepts what the day brings. He may hunker down, but he never gives in. He takes life as it comes, and that is why he survives. —DR. GEORGE SHEEHAN

Fight one more round. When your feet are so tired you have to shuffle back to the center of the ring, fight one more round. —JAMES J. CORBETT

Bear in mind, if you are going to amount to anything, that your success does not depend upon the brilliancy and the impetuosity with which you take hold, but upon the everlasting and sanctified bull-doggedness with which you hang on after you have taken hold.

—Dr. A.B. Meldrum

When you get into a tight place, and everything goes against you, till it seems as though you could not hold on a moment longer, never give up then, for that is just the place and time that the tide will turn.

—Harriet Beecher Stowe

Never let your head hang down. Never give up and sit down and grieve. Find another way. And don't pray when it rains if you don't pray when the sun shines.

—Leroy (Satchel) Paige

When nothing seems to help, I go and look at a stonecutter hammering away at his rock perhaps a hundred times without as much as a crack showing in it. Yet at the hundred and first blow it will split in two, and I know it was not that blow that did it—but all that had gone before.

—Jacob Riis

Philosophy of Life

Never bend your head. Always hold it high. Look the world straight in the eye.   —HELEN KELLER

I take a simple view of living. It is keep your eyes open and get on with it.   —LAURENCE OLIVIER

My formula for living is quite simple. I get up in the morning and I go to bed at night. In between, I occupy myself as best I can.   —CARY GRANT

So get a few laughs and do the best you can. Don't have an ideal to work for. That's like riding towards the mirage of a lake.   —WILL ROGERS

Keep walking and keep smiling.
—TINY TIM (HERBERT KHAURY)

My code of life and conduct is simply this; work hard; play to the allowable limit; disregard equally the good and bad opinion of others; never do a friend a dirty trick; . . . never grow indignant over anything; . . . live the moment to the utmost of its possibilities; . . . and be satisfied with life always, but never with oneself.   —GEORGE JEAN NATHAN

To live creatively, to live honorably, to hurt no one insofar as possible, to enjoy mortality, to fear neither death nor immortality, to cherish fools and failures even more than wise men and saints since there are more of them, to believe, to hope, to work, and to do these things with humor.   —WILLIAM SAROYAN

I have a simple philosophy. Fill what's empty. Empty what's full. And scratch where it itches.
                              —ALICE ROOSEVELT LONGWORTH

A lot of my philosophy comes from the ring. You learn in life there are always the ups and downs. We must have enough sense to enjoy our ups and enough heart to get through our downs.   —MICKEY WALKER

First health I ask, good fortune next, and third rejoicing; last, to owe nought to any man.   —PHILEMON

Walk groundly, talk profoundly, drink roundly, sleep soundly.   —WILLIAM HAZLITT

Learn to bend. It's better than breaking.
                              —ANONYMOUS

Let us not look back in anger, nor forward in fear, but around us in awareness.   —JAMES THURBER

The ideals that have lighted my way, and time after time have given me new courage to face life cheerfully, have been Kindness, Beauty and Truth.

—ALBERT EINSTEIN

Save not your best—share
Yearn for what's admirable—dare
Linger not in the past—explore

—SANDEE Y. LIN

Positive Thinking

Refuse to be ill. Never tell people you are ill; never own it to yourself. Illness is one of those things which a man should resist on principle at the onset.

—EDWARD GEORGE BULWER-LYTTON

Say you are well, or all is well with you,
And God shall hear your words and make them true.

—ELLA WHEELER WILCOX

Every day, in every way, I am getting better and better.

—EMILE COUÉ, FORMULA FOR AUTO-SUGGESTION
USED AT HIS CLINIC IN NANCY

All of a sudden, instead of feeling like a helpless victim waiting for things to get worse, I got angry, angry at the whole mess—my stomachaches, colds, constant weight loss diets, and the specter of cancer. I had had it. If I was indeed to become a cancer statistic, it wasn't going to be without a fight. In fact, I made a commitment to the universe that *I wasn't going to allow it to happen*. I would do whatever had to be done to prevent my gradual deterioration and demise. . . . I started getting excited. I knew it was going to be a long haul, but already I began to feel more positive.

—HARVEY DIAMOND

Think yourself out of getting sick. If you're getting a cold, take vitamin C, drink hot tea, and go to bed with a hot water bottle. Tell yourself, "I'll be completely well in the morning."   —JOAN BRANSTEN SUTTON

He who can believe himself well, will be well.

—OVID

To wish to be healthy is a part of being healthy.

—SENECA

If you find your inner conversation running along negative lines, you have the power to change the subject, to think along different lines.

—MARTHA SMOCK

To a healthy man, everything seems healthy.
—RUSSIAN PROVERB

The surest road to health, say what they will,
Is never to suppose we shall be ill.
Most of those evils we poor mortals know
From doctors and imagination flow.
—CHARLES CHURCHILL

The pleasantest things in the world are pleasant thoughts: and the great art of life is to have as many of them as possible. —MICHEL DE MONTAIGNE

Try to keep your mind constantly on the pleasant aspects of life and on actions which can improve your situation. Try to forget everything that is irrevocably ugly or painful. This is perhaps the most efficient way of minimizing stress. —HANS SELYE

Positive thinking usually gets you over the hump.
—ALICE GARRETT

When the world trembles I'm unmoved,
When cloudy, I'm serene;
When darkness covers all without
I'm always bright within.
—DANIEL DEFOE

All that we are is the result of what we have thought;
it is founded on our thoughts, it is made up of our
thoughts. If a man speaks or acts with a pure thought,
happiness follows him, like a shadow that never leaves
him.   —BUDDHA

Be like the bird, who halting in his flight on limb too
slight, yet sings—knowing he has wings.
                                      —VICTOR HUGO

Believe in yourself! Have faith in your abilities!
Without a humble but reasonable confidence in your
own powers you cannot be successful or happy. . . .
Formulate and stamp indelibly on your mind a mental
picture of yourself as succeeding. Hold this picture te-
naciously. Never permit it to fade. your mind will seek
to develop the picture. . . . Do not build up obstacles
in your imagination. . . . Do not be awestruck by other
people and try to copy them. Nobody can be you as ef-
ficiently as YOU can.   —NORMAN VINCENT PEALE

They can because they think they can.
                                      —VIRGIL

For they can conquer who believe they can.
                                      —RALPH WALDO EMERSON

Man is what he believes.
                                      —ANTON CHEKOV

Our belief at the beginning of a doubtful undertaking
is the one thing that insures the successful outcome of
our venture.   —WILLIAM JAMES

One's confidence, or lack of it, in the prospects of
recovery from serious illness affects the chemistry of
the body. The belief system converts hope, robust expectations, and the will to live into plus factors in any
contest of forces involving disease. . . . Everything begins, therefore, with belief. What we believe is the
most powerful option of all.   —NORMAN COUSINS

Belief is a potent medicine.
                                        —DR. STEVEN LOCKE
                                        —DOUGLAS COLLIGAN

Make yourself happy. Resolve your conflicts. Get
things off your chest. Find that peace of mind, that
clear conscience.   —DR. BERNIE SIEGEL

I wish to live without hate, whim, jealousy, envy, fear.
I wish to be simple, honest, frank, natural, clean in
mind and clean in body . . . to face any obstacle and
meet every difficulty unabashed and unafraid.
                                        —ELBERT HUBBARD

When the outlook is steeped in pessimism, I remind
myself, ''Two and two still make four, and you can't
keep mankind down for long.''   —BERNARD BARUCH

It doesn't hurt to be optimistic. You can always cry
later.   —LUCIMAR SANTOS DE LIMA

The essence of optimism is that it . . . enables a man
to hold his head high, to claim the future for himself
and not abandon it to his enemy.
                                    —DIETRICH BONHOEFFER

If we want a joyous life, we must think joyous
thoughts. If we want a prosperous life, we must think
prosperous thoughts. If we want a loving life, we must
think loving thoughts. Whatever we send out mentally
or verbally will come back to us in like form.
                                    —LOUISE L. HAY

When fate knocks you flat on your back, remember
she leaves you looking up.   —ANONYMOUS

Positiveness begets positiveness.
                                    —LEO BUSCAGLIA

I know what's happening in this world—there are liars
and cheats, there's prejudice, violence, greed, sickness
—I know what's happening. I'm not going to let it de-
ter me from living my life, though. Look, I live in this
world, and goddammit, I'm going to be cheerful and
positive about living in this world.
                                    —JOSEPH RAYMOND

The most important factor for me was a leap of faith in knowing what I wanted. It wasn't a question of *would* it work but that I was going to *make* it work.
—Dr. Richard Diamond

Always direct your thoughts to those truths that will give you confidence, hope, joy, love, thanksgiving, and turn away your mind from those that inspire you with fear, sadness, depression.
—Bertrand Wilberforce

There is a tremendous power in positive thinking. When you expect the best, you literally create a thought field that magnetizes that which you desire. Like attracts like.
—Douglas Bloch

Keep your face to the sunshine and you cannot see the shadow.
—Helen Keller

Prevention

Prevention of disease must become the goal of every physician.
—Henry E. Sigerist

The aim of medicine is to prevent disease and prolong life, the ideal of medicine is to eliminate the need of a physician.   —WILLIAM J. MAYO

The prevention of disease today is one of the most important factors in the line of human endeavor.
                    —CHARLES H. MAYO

A revolution has been slowly and quietly taking place in the attitudes of many people towards disease and health. More and more people are realizing that it is possible to create health and not just combat sickness. . . . Instead of perpetuating the notion that disease is normal, we will help create a world which affirms perfect health.   —MEIR SCHNEIDER

Thousands upon thousands of persons have studied disease. Almost no one has studied health.
                    —ADELLE DAVIS

Walking in the open is the best and most beneficial form of exercise for any age or any condition, as well as the best way to prevent disease.   —PAAVO AIROLA

There is no short-cut to longevity. To win it is the work of a lifetime, and the promotion of it is a branch of preventative medicine.
                    —JAMES CHRICHTON-BROWNE

The personality without conflict is immune from illness.   —DR. EDWARD BACH

The human mind can be trained to play an important part both in preventing disease and in overcoming it when it occurs.   —NORMAN COUSINS

Prevention is better than cure.
                              —THOMAS LOVE PEACOCK

It is of the greatest importance to prevent disease, since the cure of them by physic is so very precarious.
                              —BENJAMIN FRANKLIN

Perhaps the single most important development which favors an upsurge in interest in preventive medicine is the increasing disillusionment of the American people with health care.   —IRVING TABERSHOW

A powerful, nutritionally fit blood stream is your greatest defense against the invasion of germs.
                                    —PAUL C. BRAGG

Past thirty-five years of age and particularly past forty, the annual, comprehensive, preventive health exam is one of the most important parts of a good preventive program.   —DR. KENNETH H. COOPER

Prevention includes practices such as eating right, not smoking, avoiding environmental hazards, wearing seat belts, exercising, having safe sex, and getting medical checkups.   —ROBERT RODALE

Better than a physician is the care of health.
                              —JAPANESE PROVERB

I will prevent disease wherever I can, for prevention is preferable to cure. I will remember there is art to medicine as well as science, and that warmth, sympathy and understanding may outweigh the surgeon's knife or the chemist's drug . . .
                              —LOUIS LASAGNA, M.D.

Problems

When one's own problems are unsolvable and all best efforts frustrated, it is lifesaving to listen to other people's problems.   —SUZANNE MASSIE

Nobody, as long as he moves about among the chaotic currents of life, is without trouble.   —CARL JUNG

Have you got a problem? Do what you can where you are with what you've got.   —THEODORE ROOSEVELT

Every human being is a problem in search of a solution.   —ASHLEY MONTAGU

The measure of success is not whether you have a tough problem to deal with, but whether it's the same problem you had last year.   —JOHN FOSTER DULLES

A problem well-stated is a problem half-solved.   —CHARLES F. KETTERING

Psychiatrist

There is no psychiatrist in the world like a puppy licking your face.   —BERN WILLIAMS

Any man who goes to a psychiatrist ought to have his head examined.   —SAMUEL GOLDWYN

A psychiatrist is a fellow who asks you a lot of expensive questions your wife asks you for nothing.   —JOEY ADAMS

Psychiatry—the care of the id by the odd.

—ANONYMOUS

A neurotic is a man who builds a castle in the air. A psychotic is a man who lives in it. And a psychiatrist is the man who collects the rent.

—ROBERT WEBB-JOHNSTONE

Many a patient, after countless sessions, has quit therapy, because he could detect no perceptible improvement in his shrink's condition.   —BRENDAN FRANCIS

A psychiatrist is a man who goes to the Folies Bergère and looks at the audience.   —MERVYN STOCKWOOD

Being a good psychoanalyst, in short, has the same disadvantages as being a good parent—the children desert one as they grow up.   —MORTON HUNT

Regimen

Avoid fried meats which angry up the blood. If your stomach disputes you, lie down and pacify it with cool thoughts. Keep the juices flowing by jangling around gently as you move. Go very lightly on the vices, such as carrying on in society. The social ramble ain't restful. Avoid running at all times. Don't look back. Someone might be gaining on you.

—LEROY (SATCHEL) PAIGE

Regularity in the hours of rising and retiring, perseverance in exercise, adaption of dress to the variations of climate, simple and nutritious aliment, and temperance in all things are necessary branches of the regimen of health. —LYDIA H. SIGOURNEY

Never hurry; take plenty of exercise; always be cheerful, and take all the sleep you need, and you may expect to be well. —J.F. CLARKE

Good food, proper diet, clean water, avoiding all excesses, fresh air, ample exercise—these are what we need for a healthier life.   —Bob Ryan

Regimen is superior to medicine. Every one should be his own physician. He ought to assist, and not to force nature. Eat with moderation what agrees with your constitution. Nothing is good for the body but what we can digest. What medicine can procure digestion? Exercise. What will recruit strength? Sleep. What will alleviate incurable evils? Patience.   —Voltaire

Keeping the body totally fit and functional is no job for the uninformed or the careless person. It requires an understanding of the body, sound health and eating practices, and disciplined living. The results of such a regimen can be measured in happiness, radiant health, agelessness, peace of mind, in the joy of living and high achievement.   —Patricia Bragg

Relaxation/Rest

Work, work, work and more work is do-do. Work and relax, work and relax is do-be-do.
                    —Dr. Richard Diamond

For fast-acting relief, try slowing down.

—LILY TOMLIN

In the name of God, stop a moment, cease your work, look around you . . .   —LEO TOLSTOY

There is one piece of advice which I think no one will object to; and that is, every now and then to be completely idle—to do nothing at all.   —SYDNEY SMITH

Sit in reverie, and watch the changing color of the waves that break upon the idle seashore of the mind.

—HENRY WADSWORTH LONGFELLOW

Rest is not a matter of doing absolutely nothing. Rest is repair.   —DANIEL W. JOSSELYN

When I have nothing to do for an hour, and I don't want to do anything, I neither read nor watch television. I sit back in a chair and let my mind relax. I do what I call idling. It's as if the motorcar's running but you haven't got it in gear. You have to allow a certain amount of time in which you are doing nothing in order to have things occur to you, to let your mind think.   —MORTIMER ADLER

What is this life if, full of care,
We have no time to stand and stare?

—WILLIAM HENRY DAVIES

Too much rest itself becomes a pain.

—HOMER

Men tire themselves in pursuit of rest.

—LAURENCE STERNE

Rest is valuable only so far as it is a contrast. Pursued as an end, it becomes a most pitiable condition.

—DAVID SWING

Rest is not idleness, and to lie sometimes on the grass under the trees on a summer's day, listening to the murmur of water, or watching the clouds float across the sky, is by no means a waste of time.

—JOHN LUBBOCK

Rest in bed will do more for more diseases than any other single procedure.   —LOGAN CLENDENING

The time to relax is when you don't have time for it.

—SYDNEY J. HARRIS

Take rest; a field that has rested gives a bountiful crop.

—OVID

I loafe and invite my soul,
I lean and loafe at my ease
    observing a spear of summer grass.

—WALT WHITMAN

It is important to relax our minds as it is to concentrate them. —CHARLES B. NEWCOMB

There is no doubt that at the very onset of minor ailments, if we could but get a few hours' complete relaxation the illness would be aborted.

—DR. EDWARD BACH

Slow me down, Lord. . . . Teach me the art of taking minute vacations of slowing down. To look at a flower; to chat with an old friend or make a new one; to pat a stray dog; to watch a spider build a web; to smile at a child; or to read from a good book.

—ORIN L. CRANE

When I am losing my head and all about me are keeping theirs, when I am filled with the frustrations and anxieties of my daily routine, when I am no longer living my own life but simply reacting to others, I look for a time-out, whether it is 60 minutes or 60 seconds.

—DR. GEORGE SHEEHAN

One of our greatest statesmen has said that a change of work is the best rest. —ARTHUR CONAN DOYLE

Remedy/Solution

In the question is the solution.

—J. KRISHNAMURTI

Every problem teaches us how to resolve it.

—KAREN CASEY
—MARTHA VANCEBURG

Don't find fault. Find a remedy.

—HENRY FORD

The remedy is to find out the problem and not the cause of it. —RALPH YANELLO

Patience is the best remedy for every trouble.

—PLAUTUS

Our remedies oft in ourselves do lie,
Which we ascribe to heaven.

—SHAKESPEARE

The first step in solving a problem is to tell someone about it. —JOHN PETER FLYNN

Of all the people you will know in a lifetime, you are the only one you will never leave nor lose. To the question of your life, you are the only answer. To the problems of your life, you are the only solution.

—Jo Coudert

The remedy to physical isolation is being with others. The remedy to spiritual isolation is opening ourselves to the spirit of life and love that exists everywhere. We can be open to that spirit whether we are alone or with others.

—Amy E. Dean

[A] workable and effective way to meet and overcome difficulties is to take on someone else's problems. It is a strange fact, but you can handle two difficulties— your own and somebody else's—better than you can handle your own alone. That truth is based on a subtle law of self-giving or outgoingness whereby you develop a self-strengthening in the process.

—Norman Vincent Peale

> For every ailment under the sun,
> There is a remedy, or there is none;
> If there be one, try to find it;
> If there is none, never mind it.
>
> —Anonymous

For every human problem, there is a neat, plain solution—and it is always wrong. —H.L. Mencken

The chief cause of problems is solutions.
—ERIC SEVAREID

The best remedy for a cold is to go to bed with a good book, or a friend who's read one.   —ROD MCKUEN

Be it remembered that when the fault is found the remedy lies not in a battle against this and not in a use of will power and energy to suppress a wrong, but in a steady development of the opposite virtue. . . . For example, should there be cruelty in our nature, we can continually say, "I will not be cruel," and so prevent ourselves erring in that direction; but the success of this depends on the strength of the mind, and should it weaken we might for the moment forget our good resolve. But should we, on the other hand, develop real sympathy towards our fellow-men, this quality will once and for all make cruelty impossible. . . .
—DR. EDWARD BACH

For extreme diseases, extreme remedies.
—HIPPOCRATES

To do nothing is sometimes a good remedy.
—HIPPOCRATES

There are remedies worse than the disease.
—PUBLILIUS SYRUS

Pure air, sunlight, abstemiousness, rest, exercise, proper diet, the use of water, trust in Divine power— these are the true remedies.   —E.G. WHITE

Routine

The difference between a rut and a grave is the depth.   —GERALD BURRILL

It is not labor that kills, but the small attritions of daily routine that wear us down.   —ROY BEDICHECK

Rules for Living

I think there is one smashing rule—never face the facts.   —RUTH GORDON

Fear less, hope more; eat less, chew more; whine less, breathe more; talk less, say more; hate less, love more; and all good things are yours.   —SWEDISH PROVERB

Rules for Living

My Purpose

To awaken each morning with a smile brightening my
   face;

To greet the day with reverence for the opportunities
   it contains;

To approach my work with a clean mind;

To hold ever before me, even in the doing of little
   things, the Ultimate Purpose toward which I am
   working;

To meet men and women with laughter on my lips and
   love in my heart;

To be gentle, kind, and courteous through all the
   hours;

To approach the night with weariness that ever woos
   sleep, and the joy that comes from work well
   done—

This is how I desire to waste wisely my days.

—THOMAS DEKKER

Only two rules really count. Never miss an opportunity
to relieve yourself; never miss a chance to sit down
and rest your feet.   —DUKE OF WINDSOR

Eat a little at night, open your windows, drive out
often, and look for the good in things and people.
. . . You will no longer be sad, or bored, or ill.

—MARY KNOWLES

When you are hungry, eat; when you are tired, sleep.

—ZEN SAYING

Never put off till tomorrow what you can do today.
Never trouble another for what you can do yourself.
Never spend your money before you have it.
Never buy what you do not want because it is cheap.
Pride costs us more than hunger, thirst, and cold.
We seldom repent having eaten too little.
Nothing is troublesome that we do willingly.
How much pain the evils have cost us that have never
   happened.
Take things always by the smooth handle.
When angry, count ten before you speak; if very
   angry, a hundred.

—THOMAS JEFFERSON

1. *Stop worrying*. Worry kills life.
2. *Begin each day with a prayer*. It will arm your soul.
3. *Control appetite*. Over-indulgence clogs body and mind.
4. *Accept your limitations*. All of us can't be great.
5. *Don't envy*. It wastes time and energy.
6. *Have faith in people*. Cynicism sours the disposition.
7. *Find a hobby*. It will relax your nerves.
8. *Read a book a week* to stimulate imagination and broaden your view.
9. *Spend some time alone*, for the peace of solitude and silence.
10. *Try to want what you have*, instead of spending your strength trying to get what you want.

—ABRAHAM L. FEINBERG

Make it a rule of life never to regret and never to look back. Regret is an appalling waste of energy; you can't build on it; it's only good for wallowing in.

—KATHERINE MANSFIELD

Promise Yourself

To be so strong that nothing can disturb your peace of mind.

To talk health, happiness and prosperity to every person you meet.

To make all your friends feel that there is something in them.

To look at the sunny side of everything and make your optimism come true.

To think only of the best, to work only for the best and to expect only the best.

To be just as enthusiastic about the success of others as you are about your own.

To forget the mistakes of the past and press on to the greater achievements of the future.

To wear a cheerful countenance at all times and give every living creature you meet a smile.

To give so much time to the improvement of yourself that you have no time to criticize others.

To be too large for worry, too noble for anger, too strong for fear, and too happy to permit the presence of trouble.

—CHRISTIAN D. LARSON

Take Time for Twelve Things

1. *Take time to Work*—it is the price of success.
2. *Take time to Think*—it is the source of power.
3. *Take time to Play*—it is the secret of youth.
4. *Take time to Read*—it is the foundation of knowledge.
5. *Take time to Worship*—it is the highway of reverence and washes the dust of earth from our eyes.
6. *Take time to Help and Enjoy Friends*—it is the source of happiness.
7. *Take time to Love*—it is the one sacrament of life.
8. *Take time to Dream*—it hitches the soul to the stars.
9. *Take time to Laugh*—it is the singing that helps with life's loads.
10. *Take time for Beauty*—it is everywhere in nature.
11. *Take time for Health*—it is the true wealth and treasure of life.
12. *Take time to Plan*—it is the secret of being able to have time to take time for the first eleven things.

—PAUL C. BRAGG

I did not know I was going to live 153 years, so I don't have rules.

—SHIRIN GASONOGLY GASANOV, BORN 1817 IN AZERBAIJAN, USSR.

Running

I ran away from things all my life before I started
running.   —ANONYMOUS

If you want to live, you must walk. If you want to live
long, you must run.   —JINABHAI NAVIK

Running has given me a glimpse of the greatest freedom that a man can ever know, because it results in the
simultaneous liberation of both body and mind.
                                    —ROGER BANNISTER

Running, as every runner discovers, is not just drudgery but sport, amusement and a telephoneless, bossless
escape into freedom from everyday pressures.
                                    —JIM FIXX

People who run find their lives so much more enjoyable. Everything works better. Their cardiovascular
system. Their gastrointestinal system. Even their ability to think.   —DR. RALPH PAFFENBARGER

How much happiness is gained, and how much misery
escaped, by frequent and violent agitation of the body.
                                    —SAMUEL JOHNSON

It's a treat, being a long-distance runner.
—ALAN SILLITOE

A good run makes you feel sort of holy.
—NANCY GERSTEIN

The only reason I would take up jogging is so I could hear heavy breathing again.   —ERMA BOMBECK

Running is my doctor.
—ANONYMOUS

To know running is to know life.
—DR. GEORGE SHEEHAN

In the creative action of running, I became convinced of my own importance, certain that my life had significance.   —DR. GEORGE SHEEHAN

My every waking hour is lived as a runner. I eat as a runner. I view weather, the terrain, the environment as a runner. I see all things as positive or negative in their action on my running.   —DR. GEORGE SHEEHAN

When it's pouring with rain and you're bowling along through the wet there's a satisfaction of knowing you're out there and the others aren't.
—PETER SNELL

Running occupies but one hour of the day. Many people spend that time working on crossword puzzles.

—HAL HIGDON

Long distance running can give you a teenage cholesterol, remodel your lungs, lower your blood pressure and slow your pulse.

—DR. RICHARD STEINER

A runner once came to me and told me that he was in a 55-mile race, and at 35 miles he began to get foot cramp. He asked me what he should do. I told him to see a psychiatrist.   —MURRAY WEISENFELD, PODIATRIST

Self-Healing

The natural healing force within each one of us is the greatest force in getting well.　　　—Hippocrates

I know myself better than any doctor.

—Ovid

The placebo makes a statement that we have within us a certain self-regulatory mechanism, a self-healing mechanism, which can be mobilized given proper situational and environmental cues.　　　—David Sobel

We are now starting to collect the clues to the identity of the oldest and most reliable unseen ally of medicine. . . . The ally is the healer within each of us. And now, after centuries of being little more than a shadowy presence, a bit of medical folklore, it is beginning to reveal some of its secrets and its powers.

—Dr. Steven Locke
—Douglas Colligan

If we can begin to heal ourselves, then I believe that process can be applied to our own society and even the world at large.   —EILEEN ROCKEFELLER GROWALD

Disease can be healed, if we are willing to change the way we think and believe and act.   —LOUISE L. HAY

We must go within ourselves to heal ourselves.
—LOUISE L. HAY

People are healed by many different kinds of healers and systems because the real healer is within.
—GEORGE GOODHEART

I take all stories of miraculous healings, spontaneous remissions, and instantaneous cures as evidence for the remarkable self-healing abilities that are possible in all humanity.   —JERRY SOLFVIN

All healing, without exception, is self-healing.
—JANET F. QUINN

All acts of healing are ultimately our selves healing our Self.   —RAM DASS (RICHARD ALPERT)

We are our own healers. Our minds and bodies tell us when to eat, sleep, and relax. When we listen, we are in touch with the ways we can help ourselves feel better.   —AMY E. DEAN

It is universally admitted that there is a natural healing power resident in the body. . . . Many people have learned to relax and to keep quiet like the animals, giving nature a free opportunity to heal their maladies.

—HORATIO DRESSER

Perhaps the grandest power of health is self-healing. I say "grandest" because it's the least expensive, most accessible and, in some ways, the most potent of health forces. It's inexpensive because your body supplies it free. It's accessible because it's part of you. It's potent because through the immune defenses it can slay germs by the millions, repel countless ills, avert a hundred microscopic calamities. —ROBERT RODALE

Self-Help

No one can really pull you up very high—you lose your grip on the rope. But on your own two feet you can climb mountains. —LOUIS BRANDEIS

God gives the nuts, but He does not crack them.

—GERMAN PROVERB

God is a hard worker, but He likes to be helped.

—BASQUE PROVERB

Call on God, but row away from the rocks.
—INDIAN PROVERB

If there is no wind, row.
—LATIN PROVERB

Do not lie in a ditch and say, God help me; use the lawful tools He hath lent thee.   —GEORGE CHAPMAN

The gods help him who helps himself.
—EURIPIDES

If you will only help yourself, God will help you.
—MATHURIN REGNIER

He who is plenteously provided for from within needs but little from without.   —GOETHE

There are admirable potentialities in every human being. Believe in your strength and your youth. Learn to repeat endlessly to yourself, "It all depends on me."
—ANDRÉ GIDE

Do the hardest thing on earth for you. Act for yourself. Face the truth.   —KATHERINE MANSFIELD

Robinson had a servant even better than Friday: his name was Crusoe.   —FRIEDRICH NIETZSCHE

The next major advance in the health of the American people will result only from what the individual is willing to do for himself. —John H. Knowles

We are told what fine things would happen if every one of us would go and do something for the welfare of somebody else; but why not contemplate also the immense gain which would ensue if everybody would do something for himself? —W.G. Sumner

We can be sure that the greatest hope for maintaining equilibrium in the face of any situation rests within ourselves. Persons who are secure with a transcendental system of values and a deep sense of moral duties are possessors of values which no man and no catastrophe can take from him.

—Dr. Francis J. Braceland

Ultimately, we will be healthier, not because of new drugs or surgical techniques, but because of the things we will do for ourselves. —Louis Sullivan, M.D.

Self-Love

Above all things, reverence yourself.

—Pythagoras

If I am not for myself, who will be for me?
—ANONYMOUS

Self-respect—that cornerstone of all virtue.
—JOHN HERSCHEL

The ability to love oneself, combined with the ability to love life . . . enables one to improve the quality of life.
—DR. BERNIE SIEGEL

Indeed, to learn how to be good to oneself is often more difficult than to learn how to be good to others.
—PAUL C. BRAGG

When you cannot get a compliment any other way pay yourself one.
—MARK TWAIN

You've got to learn to like yourself first. I'm a little screwed-up, but I'm beautiful.
—STEVE MCQUEEN

I celebrate myself and sing myself.
—WALT WHITMAN

Loving yourself means giving your body the food, exercise and rest that it needs. It means listening to your feelings and asking others for what you want—without feeling guilty about it.
—DOUGLAS BLOCH

When we really love and accept and approve of ourselves exactly as we are, then everything in life works.
—LOUISE L. HAY

So how do you love yourself? First of all and most important: Cease all criticism of yourself and others. Accept yourself as you are. When you approve of yourself, your changes become positive. Everyone in your world is a reflection of your beliefs. Don't blame others; change your beliefs. Be gentle, kind and patient with yourself. Praise yourself as much as you can.
—LOUISE L. HAY

In loving myself I gain the power of identity that is necessary before love for others is possible.
—DAVID G. JONES

Be yourself. Who else is better qualified?
—FRANK J. GIBLIN, II

The man is happy, we say, who knows no good that would be greater than that which he can give to himself.
—SENECA

As a human being related to all living beings we must first be related to ourselves. We cannot understand, love and welcome others without first knowing and loving ourselves.
—JEAN KLEIN

Be who you are, not what others expect you to be.
Love who you are, and love will begin to flow in your
relationships.   —MARILYN DIAMOND

To love one's self is the beginning of a life-long
romance.   —OSCAR WILDE

Self-love is the instrument of our preservation.
                                          —VOLTAIRE

I to myself am dearer than a friend.
                                       —SHAKESPEARE

We have to learn to be our own best friends because
we fall too easily into the trap of being our worst
enemies.   —RODERICK THORP

He who falls in love with himself will have no rivals.
                                  —BENJAMIN FRANKLIN

Simplicity

It is the simple things of life—the simple things because
they are nearer the great Truth—that real pleasure is
to be found.   —DR. EDWARD BACH

Simplify, simplify, simplify. Live unknown, make your wants few. Shed this externalized clutter, these needless needs; they are merely a form of bondage and hinder man's journey.   —Robert S. de Ropp

Simplicity, simplicity, simplicity! I say, let your affairs be as two or three, and not a hundred or a thousand; instead of a million count half a dozen, and keep your accounts on your thumbnail . . . Simplify, simplify.
—Henry David Thoreau

A man is rich in proportion to the number of things he can afford to let alone.   —Henry David Thoreau

True affluence is not needing anything.
—Gary Snyder

The art of art, the glory of expression and the sunshine of the light of letters, is simplicity.
—Walt Whitman

Nothing is more simple than greatness; indeed, to be simple is to be great.   —Ralph Waldo Emerson

As I grow older, I simplify both my science and my religion. Books mean less to me; prayers mean less; potions, pills and drugs mean less; but peace, friendship, love and a life of usefulness mean more, infinitely more.   —Silas Hubbard, M.D.

Simplicity is the most difficult thing to secure in this world; it is the last limit of experience and the last effort of genius.   —GEORGE SAND (AMANDINE DUPIN)

When a thought is too weak to be expressed simply, simply drop it.   —MARQUIS DE VAUVENARGUES

Look at your own life. Has it become overly complex? Have you found yourself burdened by too many possessions or responsibilities? Take a deep breath and ask yourself, "What steps can I take to reduce the clutter so that I may live simply and joyously?"
                                                    —DOUGLAS BLOCH

Don't let your possessions possess you.
                                                    —TEDDY TRUBE

Simplicity is an exact medium between too little and too much.   —JOSHUA REYNOLDS

There is a certain majesty in simplicity which is far above all the quaintness of wit.   —ALEXANDER POPE

Sleep

There is only one thing people like that is good for them: a good night's sleep.   —Edgar Watson Howe

Health is the first muse, and sleep is the condition to produce it.   —Ralph Waldo Emerson

Sound sleep cometh of moderate eating.
                                   —Bible, Ecclesiasticus

O sleep, O gentle sleep,
Nature's soft nurse.
                                   —Shakespeare

Sleep that knits up the ravell'd sleave of care,
The death of each day's life, sore labor's bath,
Balm of hurt minds, great nature's second course,
Chief nourisher in life's feast.
                                   —Shakespeare

Sleep is the golden chain that ties health and our bodies together.   —Thomas Dekker

Immoderate sleep is rust to the soul.
                                   —Thomas Overbury

The beginning of health is sleep.

—Irish Proverb

Disease and sleep keep far apart.

—Welsh Proverb

It is common experience that a problem difficult at night is resolved in the morning after the committee of sleep has worked on it. —John Steinbeck

If you can't sleep, try walking.

—Charles Dickens

If you can't sleep, then get up and do something instead of lying there and worrying. It's the worry that gets you, not the loss of sleep. —Dale Carnegie

Put off thy cares with thy clothes; so shall thy rest strengthen thy labor, and so thy labor sweeten thy rest.

—Francis Quarles

No small art is it to sleep: It is necessary for that purpose to keep awake all day. —Friedrich Nietzsche

Give us to go blithely on our business this day, bring us to our resting beds weary and content and undishonored, and grant us in the end the gift of sleep.

—Robert Louis Stevenson

That we are not much sicker and much madder than we are is due exclusively to the most blessed and blessing of all natural graces, sleep. —ALDOUS HUXLEY

Distrust yourself, and sleep before you fight.
—DR. JOHN ARMSTRONG

Come, blessed barrier between day and day,
Dear mother of fresh thoughts and joyous health!
—WILLIAM WORDSWORTH

Six hours of sleep is enough.
—LATIN PROVERB

Nature requires five [hours],
Custom takes seven,
Idleness takes nine
And wickedness eleven.
—OLD ENGLISH RHYME

To sleep is to strain and purify our emotions, to deposit the mud of life, to calm the fever of the soul, to return into the bosom of maternal nature, thence to re-issue, healed and strong. Sleep is a sort of innocence and purification. —HENRI F. AMIEL

Healthful, soothing slumber that rests muscles, nerves, and brain is one of nature's greatest rejuvenators.
—HARVEY DIAMOND

May blessings light upon him who first invented sleep! It is food for the hungry, drink for the thirsty, heat for the cold, and cold for the hot. It is the coin that buys all things, and the balance that makes the king even with the shepherd, and the fool with the wise.

—Miguel de Cervantes

Come, sleep; O sleep! the certain knot of peace,
The baiting-place of wit, the balm of woe,
The poor man's wealth, the prisoner's release,
Th' indifferent judge between the high and low.

—Philip Sidney

The wiser the man the less he sleeps in the morning.

—Welsh Proverb

Let your sleep be necessary and healthful, not idle and expensive of time beyond the needs and conveniences of nature; and sometimes be curious to see the preparation the sun makes when he is coming forth from his chambers in the east.

—Jeremy Taylor

Smoking

Smoking kills. If you're killed, you've lost a very important part of your life.

—Brooke Shields

A person's right to smoke ends where the next person's nose begins.
—PUBLIC SERVICE ANNOUNCEMENT, WNET TV

Smoking is a shocking thing—blowing smoke out of our mouths into other people's mouths, eyes and noses. . . .
—SAMUEL JOHNSON

A custom loathsome to the eye, harmful to the brain, dangerous to the lungs, and in the black stinking fume thereof, nearest resembling the horrible Stygian smoke of the pit that is bottomless.
—JAMES I OF ENGLAND

My lungs were not made for smoking. I can no longer ignore my body's warning. I do not want to be a coughing, hacking old man. I must defeat my most debilitating weakness.
—ANONYMOUS

The strongest piece of advice I would give to any young woman is: Don't screw around, and don't smoke.
—EDWINA CURRIE

I kissed my first woman and smoked my first cigarette on the same day. I have never had time for tobacco since.
—ARTURO TOSCANINI

Fasting is the *best* way to quit smoking for good. After about two weeks of fasting all the desire for smoking will be gone.
—PAAVO AIROLA

I have never smoked in my life and look forward to a time when the world will look back with amazement and disgust to a practice so unnatural and offensive.
—George Bernard Shaw

We now know there are a hundred causes of cancer, and eighty of them are cigarettes.
—John Higginson

There is no language too strong to condemn this habit of self-destruction, suffering, and premature death.
—Harvey Diamond

More people die *every year* because of tobacco than the total number of Americans killed in World War I, World War II, and the Vietnam War *combined*!
—Harvey Diamond

Kissing a smoker is like licking an ashtray.
—Anonymous

Here is why you should not smoke. Smoking cigarettes is likely to shorten your life. . . . Smoking directly causes or contributes to the three main causes of American deaths: heart disease, cancer and accidents.
—Jane E. Brody

Smoking is pulmonary rape.
—Bumper Sticker

There are immediate benefits of quitting [smoking]: a decline in the oxygen-robbing carbon monoxide in the blood, improved sleep, the disappearance of head-aches and stomach aches . . . enhanced stamina, keener senses of taste and smell . . . and the disappear-ance of smoker's cough. —JANE E. BRODY

Soul/Spirit

Man never made any material as resilient as the human spirit. —BERN WILLIAMS

I believe that man will not merely endure: he will prevail. He is immortal, not because he alone among creatures has an inexhaustible voice, but because he has a soul, a spirit capable of compassion and sacrifice and endurance. —WILLIAM FAULKNER

Good humor is the health of the soul; sadness is its poison. —STANISLAUS LESZCYNSKI

What do you suppose will satisfy the soul, except to walk free and own no superior? —WALT WHITMAN

The principal thing in this world is to keep one's soul aloft. —GUSTAVE FLAUBERT

There is only one thing that counts in this life, and it beats all maxims ever penned—that is, for a man's spirit to be all right.   —E.W. BOK

Doctors don't know everything really. They understand matter, not spirit. And you and I live in the spirit.
                                        —WILLIAM SAROYAN

For nowhere can a mind find a retreat more full of peace or more free from care than his own soul.
                                        —MARCUS AURELIUS

The soul is dyed the color of its thoughts.
                                        —MARCUS AURELIUS

Affirmation of life is the spiritual act by which man ceases to live unreflectively and begins to devote himself to his life with reverence in order to raise it to its true value. To affirm life is to deepen, to make more inward, and to exalt the will-to-live.
                                        —ALBERT SCHWEITZER

By having reverence for life, we enter into a spiritual relation with the world.   —ALBERT SCHWEITZER

As the sculptor devotes himself to wood and stone, I would devote myself to my soul.
                                        —TOYOHIKO KAGAWA

What is soul? It's like electricity—we don't really know what it is, but it's a force that can light a room.

—RAY CHARLES

Tears are summer showers to the soul.

—ALFRED AUSTIN

To be truly healthy and vitally alive you need to do more than just eat right, exercise and consult your physician. You also need something that transcends the physical. You need a healthy spirit—a health-promoting, life-affirming attitude.

—ROBERT RODALE

Stress/Tension

Stress—the confusion created when one's mind over-rides the body's basic desire to choke the living day-lights out of some s.o.b. who desperately needs it.

—BUMPER STICKER, 1990

Every stress leaves an indelible scar, and the organism pays for its survival after a stressful situation by becom-ing a little older.   —HANS SELYE

Trying to remember too many things is certainly one of the major sources of psychological stress. I make a conscious effort to forget immediately all that is unimportant and to jot down data of possible value.

—HANS SELYE

Steps a Person Can Take to Relieve Stress
Talk it out. When something worries you, don't bottle it up. . . . *Escape for a while.* When things go wrong, it helps to escape from the painful problem for a while. . . . *Work off your anger.* Do something constructive with the pent-up energy. Pitch into some physical activity or work it out in tennis or a long walk. . . . *Do something for others.* If you feel yourself worrying about yourself all the time, try doing something for somebody else. . . . *Take one thing at a time.* Take a few of the most urgent tasks and pitch into them, one at a time, setting aside all the rest for the time being. *Shun the "superman" urge.* No one can be perfect in everything.

—SUGGESTIONS FROM THE NATIONAL MENTAL
HEALTH ASSOCIATION, REPORTED BY
DR. NEIL SOLOMON

Distract your mind when you're under pressure. Do something frivolous, nonstressful and unrelated to "real life." Watch an old movie on TV, play with your dog, do a crossword puzzle, take a long swim.

—SHARON GOLD

No matter how much pressure you feel at work, if you could find ways to relax for at least five minutes every hour, you'd be more productive. Most stress we bring on ourselves through bad habits and bad attitudes. Take a pencil and paper and write down everything in your day that produces stress, checking the aggravations that create the greatest stress. Analyze all the ways you might change these situations. If you talked with a co-worker, would it ease the stress? If you got up half an hour earlier, could you stop running and take time to walk, or even stroll? Do you exercise at least twenty minutes a day? If you don't, you should, because it will relieve stress and allow you to work and sleep better. —DR. JOYCE BROTHERS

Stress is a terrible thing; it's an intellectual wrecking ball. —BOB RYAN

The process of living is the process of reacting to stress. —DR. STANLEY J. SARNOFF

Unusual irritability, which leads to quarrels, shortens life. —ALEXANDER A. BOGOMOLETZ

Learning to self-regulate our response to stress gradually leads us to meet challenge with a sense of energy and exhilaration rather than worry and despair. —PATRICIA NORRIS

Research indicates that many modern maladies, from high blood pressure and headaches to digestive disorders and back pain, can be caused or worsened by stress. —JOAN BORYSENKO

There is more to life than increasing its speed.
—GANDHI

Success

All you need in this life is ignorance and confidence, and then success is sure. —MARK TWAIN

If one advances confidently in the direction of his dreams, and endeavors to live the life which he has imagined, he will meet with a success unexpected in common hours. —HENRY DAVID THOREAU

There is only one success—to be able to spend your life in your own way. —CHRISTOPHER MORLEY

Success comes before work only in the dictionary.
—ANONYMOUS

Success is a process, a quality of mind and way of being, an outgoing affirmation of life.　—ALEX NOBLE

The men whom I have seen succeed have always been cheerful and hopeful, who went about their business with a smile on their faces, and took the changes and chances of this mortal life like men.
—CHARLES KINGSLEY

Never continue in a job you don't enjoy. If you're happy in what you're doing, you'll like yourself, you'll have inner peace. And if you have that, along with physical health, you will have had more success than you could possibly have imagined.
—JOHNNY CARSON

A man is a success if he gets up in the morning and goes to bed at night and in between does what he wants to do.　—BOB DYLAN

Success is a trendy word. Don't aim for success if you want it; just do what you love and it will come naturally.　—DAVID FROST

I can give you a six-word formula for success: "Think things through—then follow through."
—EDWARD (EDDIE) RICKENBACKER

When you get right down to the root of the meaning of the word "succeed," you find it simply means to follow through. —F.W. Nichol

To succeed, keep on doing what it took to get started.
—Anonymous

To follow, without halt, one aim: There's the secret to success. —Anna Pavlova

Put your heart, mind, intellect and soul even to your smallest acts. This is the secret of success.
—Swami Sivananda

I cannot give you the formula for success, but I can give you the formula for failure—try to please everybody. —Herbert Bayard Swope

Success is to be measured not so much by the position that one has reached in life as by the obstacles which [were] overcome while trying to succeed.
—Booker T. Washington

Success is that old ABC—ability, breaks and courage.
—Charles Luckman

If at first you don't succeed, you are running about average. —M.H. Alderson

Success, as I see it, is a result, not a goal.
—GUSTAVE FLAUBERT

Success is a journey, not a destination.
—BEN SWEETLAND

Success comes in cans; failure in can'ts.
—ANONYMOUS

Always bear in mind that your own resolution to succeed is more important than any one thing.
—ABRAHAM LINCOLN

Making a success of the job at hand is the best step toward the kind you want.   —BERNARD BARUCH

Surgery

Surgery is always second best. If you can do something else, it's better.   —DR. JOHN KIRKLIN

Surgery is the cry of defeat in medicine.
—MARTIN H. FISCHER

The practice of medicine is a thinker's art, the practice of surgery a plumber's.   —MARTIN H. FISCHER

All practice is theory; all surgery is practice; ergo, all surgery is theory.   —LANFRANC

The best surgeon is he that has been well hacked himself.   —OLD PROVERB

Swimming

When you swim you use most of the big muscle groups in your body, yet swimming doesn't place undue strain on your joints.   —DR. JAMES E. COUNSILMAN

Floating along, breathing deeply, stroking rhythmically through the water—what a beautiful sport swimming is.   —KATHERINE VAZ
—CHIP ZEMPEL

It is a good idea to begin at the bottom in everything except in learning to swim.   —ANONYMOUS

Talent

Whatever you are by nature, keep to it; never desert your line of talent. Be what nature intended you for and you will succeed. —SYDNEY SMITH

If you have a talent, use it in every which way possible. Don't hoard it. Don't dole it out like a miser. Spend it lavishly like a millionaire intent on going broke. —BRENDAN FRANCIS

Hide not your talents, they for use were made.
What's a Sun-dial in the Shade?
—BENJAMIN FRANKLIN

Work while you have the light. You are responsible for the talent that has been entrusted to you.
—HENRI F. AMIEL

Toil to make yourself remarkable by some talent or other. —SENECA

Use what talents you possess: the woods would be very silent if no birds sang there except those that sang best.   —HENRY VAN DYKE

If you have talent, you will receive some measure of success—but only if you persist.   —ISAAC ASIMOV

He who is born with a talent, for a talent, finds in it his happiest existence.   —GOETHE

Thirst

Whoever is master of his thirst is master of his health.
                              —FRENCH PROVERB

He that goes to bed thirsty rises healthy.
                              —GEORGE HERBERT

Time

Health is the thing that makes you feel that now is the best time of the year.   —FRANKLIN P. ADAMS

I went on a diet, swore off drinking and heavy eating, and in fourteen days I lost two weeks.

—Joe E. Lewis

He who have no time for our health today, may have no health for our time tomorrow.   —Anonymous

One always has time enough, if only one applies it well.   —Goethe

You can't turn back the clock. But you can wind it up again.   —Bonnie Prudden

The time is always right to do what is right.

—Martin Luther King, Jr.

There is a time to let things happen and a time to make things happen.   —Hugh Prather

Time is the coin of your life. It is the only coin you have, and only you can determine how it will be spent. Be careful lest you let other people spend it for you.

—Carl Sandburg

A man who dares to waste one hour of time has not discovered the value of life.   —Charles Darwin

Why kill time when you can employ it?

—French Proverb

Time wasted is existence; used is life.

—EDWARD YOUNG

Time doesn't turn you into a stereotype. Whatever you were at 40, you'll be at 60 or 70, but more so. More yourself. If you're cranky, you'll be crankier; if you're an optimist, you'll hang in there.

—NANCY MCINTYRE

Time goes, you say? Ah no, alas, time stays, we go.

—AUSTIN DOBSON

Life and time are our only real possessions.

—RAY L. WILBUR

Time is an herb that cures all diseases.

—BENJAMIN FRANKLIN

Time deals gently only with those who take it gently.

—ANATOLE FRANCE

Time is lost when we have not lived a full human life, time unenriched by experience, creative endeavor, enjoyment, and suffering.   —DIETRICH BONHOEFFER

Lost, yesterday, somewhere between sunrise and sunset, two golden hours, each set with sixty diamond minutes. No reward is offered, for they are gone forever.   —HORACE MANN

Those who make the worst use of their time most complain of its shortness.　　　—JEAN DE LA BRUYÈRE

Those who do not know how to spend their time profitably allow their lives to slip away with much sorrow and little praise.　　　—ISABELLA D'ESTE

The art of medicine is generally a question of time.
　　　　　　　　　　　　　　　　　　—OVID

Time heals what reason cannot.

　　　　　　　　　　　　　　　　　—SENECA

Who hath time hath life.

　　　　　　　　　　　　　　—JOHN FLORIO

Troubles

Drag your thoughts away from your troubles—by the ears, by the heels, or any other way you can manage it. It's the healthiest thing a body can do.
　　　　　　　　　　　　　　　—MARK TWAIN

I am an old man and have known a great many troubles, but most of them have never happened.
　　　　　　　　　　　　　　　—MARK TWAIN

Troubles, like babies, grow larger by nursing.
—LADY HOLLAND

Trouble knocked at the door, but hearing a laugh within hurried away.   —ANONYMOUS

> Pack up your troubles in your old kit-bag,
> And smile, smile, smile.
> —GEORGE ASAF

Trouble is to man what rust is to iron.
—JEWISH PROVERB

When you dig another out of trouble, you find a place to bury your own.   —ANONYMOUS

Why hoard your troubles? They have no market value, so just throw them away.   —ANN SCHADE

> Better never trouble Trouble
> Until Trouble troubles you;
> For you only make your trouble
> Double-trouble when you do.
> —DAVID KEPPEL

A trouble shared is a trouble halved.
—OLD PROVERB

Understanding

Everything that irritates us about others can lead us to an understanding of ourselves.　　　—Carl Jung

I observe myself and so I come to know others.
　　　　　　　　　　　　　　　　—Lao-tse

The world is a looking glass, and gives back to every man the reflection of his own face.
　　　　　　　—William Makepeace Thackeray

Seeing imperfection in others is a mirror of our own imperfection.　　　—Joseph Raymond

That which we understand, we can't blame.
　　　　　　　　　　　　　　　　—Goethe

The best way to be understood is to be understanding.
　　　　　　　　　　　　　　　—Anonymous

Understanding will bring you compassion.
>—Louise L. Hay

Our dignity is not what we do, but in what we understand. —George Santayana

We come. We go. And in between we try to understand. —Rod Steiger

Variety

Human nature craves a certain amount of variety. We plant several kinds of flowers in our gardens. We enjoy our meals most when the selection of food is varied from day to day. The same principle applies to our daily activities. —HAROLD SHRYOCK

Variety's the very spice of life.

—WILLIAM COWPER

Variety is the mother of enjoyment.

—BENJAMIN DISRAELI

No pleasure lasts long unless there is variety in it.

—PUBLILIUS SYRUS

It takes all sorts to make a world.

—ENGLISH PROVERB

Vegetarianism

I have no doubt that it is a part of the destiny of the human race, in its gradual improvement, to leave off eating animals, as surely as the savage tribes have left off eating each other when they came in contact with the more civilized. —HENRY DAVID THOREAU

There is no disease, bodily or mental, which adoption of vegetable diet and pure water has not infallibly mitigated, wherever the experiment has been fairly tried. —PERCY BYSSHE SHELLEY

Think of the fierce energy concentrated in an acorn! You bury it in the ground, and it explodes into a giant oak! Bury a sheep, and nothing happens but decay! —GEORGE BERNARD SHAW

A man of spiritual intensity does not eat corpses. —GEORGE BERNARD SHAW

Vegetarianism is a more economical, healthful and ecologically sound way to eat. —ANONYMOUS

You put a baby in a crib with an apple and a rabbit. If it eats the rabbit and plays with the apple, I'll buy you a new car. —HARVEY DIAMOND

People often say that humans have always eaten animals, as if this is a justification for continuing the practice. According to this logic, we should not try to prevent people from murdering other people, since this has also been done since the earliest of times.

—ISAAC BASHEVIS SINGER

Animal flesh should certainly be avoided; first, because it gives rise to much physical poison in the body; secondly, because it stimulates an abnormal and excessive appetite; and thirdly, because it necessitates cruelty to the animal world.   —DR. EDWARD BACH

Vegetarianism is harmless enough, though it is apt to fill a man with wind and self righteousness.

—ROBERT HUTCHINSON

The transition to vegetarianism constitutes a critical step in the evolutionary process.

—RUDOLPH BALLENTINE

Waking

Getting up before daybreak makes for health, wealth and wisdom.　　　　　　　　　—Aristotle

Early rising maketh a man whole in body, wholer in soul, and richer in goods.　　　　—John Fitzherbert

> Early to bed and early to rise,
> Makes a man healthy, wealthy and wise.
> 　　　　　　　　　　—Benjamin Franklin

> Early to rise and early to bed,
> Makes a male healthy, wealthy and dead.
> 　　　　　　　　　　—James Thurber

Early to bed and early to rise, and you'll meet very few of our best people.　　　　　　—George Ade

If thou art sluggish on arising, let this thought occur:
I am rising to a man's work.   —MARCUS AURELIUS

Better to get up late and be wide awake than to get up
early and be asleep all day.   —ANONYMOUS

The early bird catches the worm.
                                —WILLIAM CAMDEN

I have, all my life long, been lying till noon; yet I tell
all young men, and tell them with great sincerity, that
nobody who does not rise early will ever do any good.
                                —SAMUEL JOHNSON

The average, healthy, well-adjusted adult gets up at
seven-thirty in the morning feeling just plain terrible.
                                —JEAN KERR

Rise with the lark, and go to bed with the lamb.
                                —ENGLISH PROVERB

Lying late in the morning is never found in company
with longevity. It also tends to make people corpulent.
                                —LEIGH HUNT

Walking

I have two doctors, my left leg and my right. When body and mind are out of gear I know that I shall have only to call in my doctors and I shall be well again.
—GEORGE MACAULAY TREVELYAN

I never knew a man go for an honest day's walk for whatever reason, great or small . . . and not have his reward in the repossession of his own soul.
—GEORGE MACAULAY TREVELYAN

Never have I thought so much, never have I realized my own existence so much, never have I been so much alive than when walking.   —JEAN JACQUES ROUSSEAU

A walker is a man returned to the first principles, in direct contact and intercourse with the earth and the elements, his faculties unsheathed, his mind plastic, his body toughened, his heart light, his soul dilated.
—JOHN BURROUGHS

I enjoy my legs crunching the pebbles under my feet— the way I used to enjoy crunching a crust of bread when I had teeth.   —BERNARD BERENSON

I like long walks, especially when they're taken by people who annoy me.   —FRED ALLEN

It is solved by walking.

—LATIN PROVERB

The sovereign invigorator of the body is exercise, and of all the exercises walking is best. Habituate yourself to walk very far.   —THOMAS JEFFERSON

Walking is the only exercise where you can commune more with nature and/or other human beings while actually doing that exercise.   —JOSEPH RAYMOND

Walking is the most civilized and civilizing exercise because it is the one most conducive to thinking. Other exercises do not provoke or even permit interesting thought. Imagine what the world might have lost if Kant had been a jogger or Dickens had taken up tennis.

—GEORGE F. WILL

The [English] literary movement at the end of the eighteenth century was obviously due in great part, if not mainly, to the renewed practice of walking.

—LESLIE STEPHEN

Thoughts come clearly while one walks.

—THOMAS MANN

An early morning walk is a blessing for the whole day.
—HENRY DAVID THOREAU

I keep myself in puffect shape. I get lots of exercise—in my own way—and I walk every day. . . . Knolls, you know, small knolls, they're very good for walking. Build up your muscles, going up and down knolls.
—MAE WEST

Walking makes for a long life.
—HINDU PROVERB

Manhattan might be the healthiest place in America because people walk many blocks each day.
—JIMMY BRESLIN

The soul of walking is liberty, perfect liberty, to think, feel, do just as one pleases.   —WILLIAM HAZLITT

The sum of the whole is this: walk and be happy; walk and be healthy. The best way to lengthen out our days is to walk steadily and with a purpose. The wandering man knows of certain ancients, far gone in years, who have staved off infirmities and dissolution by earnest walking—hale fellows, close upon ninety, but brisk as boys.   —CHARLES DICKENS

Walking is the favorite sport of the good and the wise.
—A.L. ROWSE

Walk forty blocks every day. Saturdays and Sundays, too. It doesn't matter how long it takes, just get into the habit of forty blocks every day.

—85-YEAR-OLD MAN ON THE STREETS OF
SAN FRANCISCO

You can rate a man's curiosity about his world and his fellow men by his walking habits.   —HAL BORLAND

Walking isn't a lost art—one must, by some means, get to the garage.   —EVEN ESAR

A walker is moving his arms, looking at the scenery, moving his muscles, using his lungs, thinking large and small thoughts, his heart is thumping, and all told, he is alive like at no other time.   —JOSEPH SUTTON

A conservative is a man with two perfectly good legs who has never learned to walk.

—FRANKLIN D. ROOSEVELT

Take a two-mile walk every morning before breakfast.

—HARRY S. TRUMAN, WHEN ASKED HIS
PRESCRIPTION FOR A LONGER LIFE

I like walking, and if I do it every day, I have no problems.   —DON NELSON

Even walking the same route each day can be interesting—just take a look around. You are moving at a pace where you begin to notice things you never saw before, changes in the scene, changes in the people who live and work along the way, seasonal changes in the light and colors, and changes in the goings-on in the neighborhood. —BLUE CROSS OF CALIFORNIA

I can walk the same path, day after day, and always uncover new glories of the creation. Over the sharply divided seasons I study the stone walls, that used to keep sheep out of corn, as they extend into dense woods. I contemplate thick-waisted matronly birches, dark hemlocks, and every spring the fragile indomitable ferns. Streams hurtle after rain and turn into the dry stony gulches of August. Snow decorates, leaves fall, moss blossoms—and I walk each day through an anthology of natural growth, change, and stasis.
—DONALD HALL

So fresh and exciting this walk up the road with haversack on my back. . . . Off all the wife, the mother, the lover, the teacher, and the violent artist takes over. I am alone. I belong to no one but myself. I mate with no one but the spirit. I own no land, have no kind, no friend or enemy. I have no road but this one.
—SYLVIA ASHTON-WARNER

Above all, do not lose your desire to walk.
—SÖREN KIERKEGAARD

For me, a long five or six mile walk helps. And one must go alone and every day. I have done this for many years. It is at these times I seem to get recharged.   —BRENDA UELAND

If you walk backward you'll find out that you can go forward and people won't know if you're coming or going.   —CASEY STENGEL

A sedentary life is the real sin against the Holy Spirit. Only those thoughts that come by walking have any value.   —FRIEDRICH NIETZSCHE

> Walking is the only exercise
> Where you can philosophize.
> 　　　　　　　　—GEORGE KREVSKY

Just suppose you found yourself walking five miles a day. Not all at once, mind you, but a little in the morning, a walk at lunch, a trip to the post office; later a walk part of the way home, even down to a restaurant or the movies in the evening and then home again. Find yourself noticing cloud formations or swifts spiraling down into the library chimney, bats flashing under a streetlight. Check the bookstores, the notices stapled to telephone poles. Find that faces are considerably more interesting than bumper stickers.
　　　　　　　　—JOHN P. WILEY, JR.

Walking dusts the cobwebs from my mind.

—JEANNIE SUTTON

How many times have I started out to walk somewhere, feeling tired and irritable, begun to think the
whole idea was a dumb mistake, then found that
despite myself the slump was even coming out of my
shoulders.   —JOHN P. WILEY, JR.

No other form of exercise is comparable to a daily
walk in the open air.   —DR. ALVAH H. DOTY

The fact is, running a marathon doesn't make you any
healthier than walking three miles three times a week
at a fairly fast pace.   —CHARLOTTE A. TATE, PH.D.

Wealth

It is health which is real wealth and not pieces of gold
and silver.   —GANDHI

Some people lose their health gaining wealth and then
lose their wealth regaining health.   —ANONYMOUS

All wealth is founded on health. To squander money
is foolish; to squander health is murder in the second
degree.   —B.C. FORBES

Health and good estate of body are above all gold, and
a strong body above infinite wealth.
                              —BIBLE, ECCLESIASTICUS

Better is a poor man healthy in body than a rich man
stricken in his flesh.   —BIBLE, ECCLESIASTICUS

Gold that buys health can never be ill spent
Nor hours laid out in harmless merriment.
                              —JOHN WEBSTER
                              —THOMAS DEKKER

The only way for a rich man to be healthy is by exercise and abstinence, to live as if he was poor; which are
esteemed the worst parts of poverty.
                              —WILLIAM TEMPLE

He who has his health is rich, and does not know it.
                              —ITALIAN PROVERB

Man is not a savage or a pauper by the inexorable
fatality of his nature. He is surrounded with every form
of the truest and noblest wealth—wealth, or well-
being, for the body, wealth for the mind, wealth for
the heart.   —HORACE MANN

Will

Will is the master of the world. Those who want something, those who know what they want, even those who want nothing, but want it badly, govern the world. —FERDINAND BRUNETIÈRE

You can have anything you want if you want it desperately enough. You must want it with an inner exuberance that erupts through the skin and joins the energy that created the world. —SHEILAH GRAHAM

Our character is our will, for what we will we are. —ARCHBISHOP MANNING

Nothing is impossible; there are ways that lead to everything, and if we had sufficient will we should always have sufficient means. It is often merely for an excuse that we say things are impossible. —LA ROCHEFOUCAULD

Where there's a will, there's a way. —ENGLISH PROVERB

When the will is ready the feet are light. —GEORGE HERBERT

I think it rather fine, this necessity for the tense bracing of the will before anything worth doing can be done.   —ARNOLD BENNETT

People do not lack strength; they lack will.
    —VICTOR HUGO

There is no power in man greater to effect anything than a will determined to exert its utmost force.
    —RICHARD CUMBERLAND

Your heaviest artillery [in sickness] will be your will to live. Keep that big gun going.   —NORMAN COUSINS

Wisdom

The growth of wisdom may be gauged accurately by the decline of ill-temper.   —FRIEDRICH NIETZSCHE

To be a philosopher is not merely to have subtle thoughts, nor even to found a school, but so to love wisdom as to live, according to its dictates, a life of simplicity, independence, magnanimity, and trust.
    —HENRY DAVID THOREAU

The most certain sign of wisdom is a continual cheerfulness; her state is like that of things in the regions above the moon, always clear and serene.

—MICHEL DE MONTAIGNE

The art of being wise is the art of knowing what to overlook.

—WILLIAM JAMES

Besides the noble art of getting things done, there is the noble art of leaving things undone. The wisdom of life consists in the elimination of nonessentials.

—LIN YUTANG

The wise man doesn't give the right answers, he poses the right questions.

—CLAUDE LEVI-STRAUSS

No man really becomes a fool until he stops asking questions.

—CHARLES P. STEINMETZ

A wise man changes his mind, a fool never.

—SPANISH PROVERB

Let us make haste to live, since every day to a wise man is a new life.

—SENECA

We learn wisdom from failure much more than from success.

—SAMUEL SMILES

Better be wise by the misfortunes of others than by
your own. —AESOP

The purpose of maintaining the body in good health
is to acquire wisdom. —MAIMONIDES

Wise people, even though all laws were abolished,
would still lead the same lives. —ARISTOPHANES

The wise don't expect to find life worth living; they
make it that way. —ANONYMOUS

Clever men are impressed in their differences from
their fellows. Wise men are conscious of their resemblance to them. —R.H. TAWNEY

The wise man is astonished by anything.
—ANDRE GIDE

The latter part of a wise man's life is taken up in curing the follies, prejudices, and false opinions he had
contracted in the former. —JONATHAN SWIFT

Pride only breeds quarrels; but wisdom is found in
those who take advice. —BIBLE, PROVERBS

He who walks with the wise grows wise, but a companion of fools suffers harm. —BIBLE, PROVERBS

Honesty is the first chapter in the book of wisdom.
—THOMAS JEFFERSON

Wisdom consists of the anticipation of consequences.
—NORMAN COUSINS

You have to raise yourself above things instead of letting things raise themselves above you.
—JAMES STEPHENS

Keep the gold and keep the silver, but give us wisdom.
—ARABIAN PROVERB

To conquer fear is the beginning of wisdom.
—BERTRAND RUSSELL

If one is too lazy to think, too vain to do a thing badly, too cowardly to admit it, one will never attain wisdom.
—CYRIL CONNOLLY

It is wisdom to believe the heart.
—GEORGE SANTAYANA

He who knows others is learned. He who knows himself is wise.
—LAO-TSE

Wisdom denotes the pursuing of the best ends by the best means.
—FRANCES HUTCHESON

The best and safest thing is to keep a balance in your life, acknowledge the great powers around us and in us. If you can do that, and live that way, you are really a wise man.   —EURIPEDES

All human wisdom is summed up in two words: wait and hope.   —ALEXANDRE DUMAS

Wisdom entereth not into a malicious mind.
                                         —RABELAIS

Professing themselves to be wise, they became fools.
                                    —BIBLE, ROMANS

The wisest man is he who does not believe that he is.
                                  —NICOLAS BOILEAU

Only madmen and fools are pleased with themselves; no wise man is good enough for his own satisfaction.
                              —BENJAMIN WHICHCOTE

A wise man will make more opportunities than he finds.   —FRANCIS BACON

Work

Employment is nature's physician, and is essential to human happiness. —GALEN

Work, man, work. If you don't give the brain some work to do, it'll dream up its own stuff—bad stuff. —BOB RYAN

To have meaningful work is a tremendous happiness. —RITA MAE BROWN

A little labor, much health. —GEORGE HERBERT

Working at your calling is half praying. —LATIN PROVERB

Only work which is the product of inner compulsion can have spiritual meaning. —WALTER GROPIUS

Blessed is he who has found his work; let him ask no other blessedness. He has a work, a life-purpose; he has found it, and will follow it. —THOMAS CARLYLE

It is work—work that one delights in—that is the surest guarantor of happiness. —ASHLEY MONTAGU

What is the use of health, or of life, if not to do some work therewith? —THOMAS CARLYLE

Work is the grand cure for all the maladies and miseries that ever beset mankind—honest work, which you intend getting done. —THOMAS CARLYLE

The more I want to get something done, the less I call it work. —RICHARD BACH

Just as there are no little people or unimportant lives, there is no insignificant work. —ELENA BONNER

I'm not sorry for anyone's being poor; I'm only sorry when they have no work. —HELENA MORLEY

The reward of labor is life.

—WILLIAM MORRIS

The highest reward for man's toil is not what he gets for it but what he becomes by it. —JOHN RUSKIN

When men are rightly occupied their amusement grows out of their work as the color-petals out of a fruitful flower. —JOHN RUSKIN

In order that people may be happy in their work, these three things are needed—they must be fit for it; they must not do too much of it; and they must have a sense of success in it.   —JOHN RUSKIN

Nothing is really work unless you would rather be doing something else.   —JAMES M. BARRIE

St. Francis of Assisi was hoeing his garden when someone asked what he would do if he were suddenly to learn that he would die before sunset that very day. "I would finish hoeing my garden," he replied.
   —LOUIS FISCHER

The day is always his who works in it with serenity and great aims.   —RALPH WALDO EMERSON

Work banishes those three great evils: boredom, vice, and poverty.   —VOLTAIRE

Work is much more fun than fun.
   —NOEL COWARD

If you have a job without aggravations, you don't have a job.   —MALCOLM S. FORBES

The test of a vocation is the love of the drudgery it involves.   —LOGAN PEARSALL SMITH

I am a great believer in luck, and I find the harder I work the more I have of it.   —THOMAS JEFFERSON

Genius is one percent inspiration and ninety-nine percent perspiration.   —THOMAS EDISON

Genius is often a short way of spelling hard work.
—B.C. FORBES

Anyone can do any amount of work, provided it isn't the work he is supposed to be doing at the moment.
—ROBERT BENCHLEY

All work and no play makes Jack a dull boy.
—JAMES HOWELL

I think that there is far too much work done in the world, that immense harm is caused by the belief that work is virtuous, and that what needs to be preached in modern industrial countries is quite different from what always has been preached.
—BERTRAND RUSSELL

Labor conquers everything.
—VIRGIL

If you wish to be at rest, labor.
—BROTHER GILES OF ASSISI

Thank God every morning when you get up that you have something to do that day which must be done, whether you like it or not. Being forced to work and forced to do your best will breed in you temperance and self-control, diligence and strength of will, cheerfulness and content, and a hundred virtues which the idle never know. —CHARLES KINGSLEY

The best part of one's life is the working part, the creative part. Believe me, I love to succeed. However, the real spiritual and emotional excitement is in the doing. —GARSON KANIN

There is dignity in work only when it is work freely accepted. —ALBERT CAMUS

How much easier our work would be if we put forth as much effort trying to improve the quality of it as most of us do trying to find excuses for not properly attending to it. —GEORGE W. BALLINGER

I don't like work. No man does. But I like what is in work—the chance to find yourself, your own reality —for yourself, not for others—what no other man can ever know. —JOSEPH CONRAD

Health lies in labor, and there is no royal road to it but through toil. —WENDELL PHILLIPS

Employment gives health, sobriety, and morals.
—DANIEL WEBSTER

Don't worry and fret, faint-hearted,
  The chances have just begun,
For the best jobs haven't been started,
  The best work hasn't been done.
—BERTON BRALEY

Worry

Worms eat you when you're dead; worries eat you
when you're alive.   —JEWISH PROVERB

God did not make us to be eaten by anxiety, but to
walk erect, free, unafraid in a world where there is
work to do, truth to seek, love to give and win.
—JOSEPH FORT NEWTON

To avoid illness, eat less. To have long life, worry less.
—CHINESE PROVERB

Don't worry, be happy.
—MEHER BABA

A hundred load of worry will not pay an ounce of debt. —George Herbert

Worry is interest paid on trouble before it becomes due. —Dean William Ralph Inge

It is not work that kills but worry. —English Proverb

I've never met a healthy person who worried much about his health, or a good person who worried much about his soul. —John B.S. Haldane

Worry often gives small things a big shadow. —Swedish Proverb

If the grass is greener in the other fellow's yard, let him worry about cutting it. —Fred Allen

How much pain the evils have cost us that have never happened. —Thomas Jefferson

Hungry Joe collected lists of fatal diseases and arranged them in alphabetical order so that he could put his finger without delay on any one he wanted to worry about. —Joseph Heller

Worry is the worst form of suicide. It is a slow form of self-destruction. —BERNARD JENSEN

One hour of worry is one hour of hell. —JAMES E. DODDS

Worry affects the circulation, the heart, the glands, the whole nervous system. —CHARLES H. MAYO

Stop all the worry. Most of what you are worried about you'll have difficulty remembering a week later. —ANONYMOUS

The reason why worry kills more people than work is that more people worry than work. —ROBERT FROST

When you worry, you go over the same ground endlessly and come out the same place you started. —HAROLD B. WALKER

Worry is a thin stream of fear trickling through the mind. If encouraged, it cuts a channel into which all other thoughts are drained. —ARTHUR SOMERS ROCHE

Only one type of worry is correct: to worry because you worry too much. —JEWISH PROVERB

Worry a little bit every day and in a lifetime you will lose a couple of years. If something is wrong, fix it if you can. But train yourself not to worry. Worry never fixes anything. —MARY HEMINGWAY

Rule number one is: "Don't sweat the small stuff." Rule number two is: "It's all small stuff." And if you can't fight and you can't flee, flow.
—DR. ROBERT S. ELIOT

How many cares one loses when one decides not to be something, but to be someone.
—GABRIELLE "COCO" CHANEL

Yesterday, Today, Tomorrow

Tomorrow's life is too late; live today.

—MARTIAL

One today is worth two tomorrows.

—FRANCIS QUARLES

One hour today is worth two tomorrow.

—THOMAS FULLER

It may be a fire today, but tomorrow it will be only ashes. —ARABIAN PROVERB

Today gold, tomorrow dust.

—DANISH PROVERB

Let us not bankrupt our todays by paying interest on the regrets of yesterday and by borrowing in advance the troubles of tomorrow. —RALPH W. SOCKMAN

Today is the pupil of yesterday.

—PUBLILIUS SYRUS

Leave tomorrow till tomorrow.

—GERMAN PROVERB

Never put off until tomorrow what you can do today.

—ENGLISH PROVERB

You had better live your best and act your best and think your best today; for today is the sure preparation for tomorrow and all the other tomorrows that follow.

—HARRIET MARTINEAU

Tomorrow doesn't matter for I have lived today.

—HORACE

I have no Yesterdays,
Time took them away;
Tomorrow may not be—
But I have Today.

—PEARL YEADON McGINNIS

Anyone who limits her vision to memories of yesterday is already dead.   —LILY LANGTRY

Light tomorrow with to-day!

—ELIZABETH BARRETT BROWNING

Today is yesterday's tomorrow.

—Michael Makowsky

There is no distance on this earth as far away as yesterday.

—Robert Nathan

One of the most tragic things I know about human nature is that all of us tend to put off living. We are all dreaming of some magical rose garden over the horizon—instead of enjoying the roses that are blooming outside our windows today.   —Dale Carnegie

Procrastination is the art of keeping up with yesterday.

—Don Marquis

It's true that tomorrow may be better—or worse. But today may not be so bad. You must appreciate the miracle that you're alive right now and forget about how, or if, you're going to live tomorrow.

—Rod Steiger

Our todays and yesterdays
Are the blocks with which we build.

—Henry Wadsworth Longfellow

There are two days about which nobody should ever worry, and these are yesterday and tomorrow.

—R.J. Burdette

He is only rich who owns today.

—RALPH WALDO EMERSON

Yesterday is a cancelled check; tomorrow is a promissory note; today is the only cash you have—so spend it wisely. —KAY LYONS

> Look to this day!
> For it is life, the very life of life. . . .
> For yesterday is but a dream
> And tomorrow is only a vision
> But today, well lived,
>   makes every yesterday
>   a dream of happiness
> And every tomorrow a vision of hope.
> Look well, therefore, to this day!
>
> —KALIDASA

The goodness that thou mayest do this day, do it; and delay it not till tomorrow. —GEOFFREY CHAUCER

Tomorrow is endless.

—RUSSIAN PROVERB

Begin now—not tomorrow, not next week, but today —to seize the moment and make this day count. Remember, yesterday is gone and tomorrow may never come. Today is all we have.

—ELLEN KREIDMAN

Finish every day and be done with it. You have done what you could. Some blunders and absurdities no doubt crept in; forget them as soon as you can. Tomorrow is a new day; begin it well and serenely and with too high a spirit to be cumbered with your old nonsense. This day is all that is good and fair. It is too dear, with its hopes and invitations, to waste a moment on the yesterdays. —RALPH WALDO EMERSON

Young and Old

You are as young as your faith, as old as your doubt; as young as your self-confidence, as old as your fear; as young as your hope, as old as your despair.
—SAMUEL ULLMAN

Spring is wonderful. It makes you feel young enough to do all the things you're old enough to know you can't. —FRANKLIN P. JONES

The sense of well-being! It's often with us
When we are young, but then it's not noticed;
And by the time one has grown to consciousness
It comes less often.
—T.S. ELIOT

When I was young, I pitied the old. Now old, it is the young I pity. —JEAN ROSTAND

You're never too old to become younger. —MAE WEST

Young. Old. Just words. —GEORGE BURNS

Whenever a man's friends begin to compliment him about looking young, he may be sure that they think he is growing old. —WASHINGTON IRVING

Nothing seems so tragic to one who is old as the death of one who is young, and this alone proves that life is a good thing. —ZÖE ATKINS

If we keep well and cheerful we are always young, and at last die in youth, even when years would count us old. —TRYON EDWARDS

We are happier in many ways when we are old than when we were young. The young sow wild oats. The old grow sage. —WINSTON CHURCHILL

To be seventy years young is sometimes far more cheerful and hopeful than to be forty years old. —OLIVER WENDELL HOLMES, SR.

Never have I enjoyed youth so thoroughly as I have in
my old age.   —GEORGE SANTAYANA

Forty is the old age of youth; fifty is the youth of old
age.   —VICTOR HUGO

Young men think old men are fools, but old men know
young men are fools.   —GEORGE CHAPMAN

Young men want to be faithful and are not; old men
want to be faithless and cannot.   —OSCAR WILDE

In youth we believe many things that are not true; in
old age we doubt many truths.   —GERMAN PROVERB

The old man shows what the young man was.
                                —SWEDISH PROVERB

The excesses of our youth are drafts upon our old age,
payable with interest, about thirty years after date.
                                —C.C. COLTON

If you don't want to get old, hang yourself while
young.   —JEWISH PROVERB

I haven't asked you to make me young again. All I want
is to go on getting older.
              —KONRAD ADENAUER, REPLYING TO HIS DOCTOR

Bibliography

Adams A.K. *The Home Book of Humorous Quotations*. New York: Dodd, Mead and Co., 1969.

Adams, Franklin Pierce. *FPA Book of Quotations*. New York: Funk and Wagnalls, 1952.

Agel, Jerome and Walter D. Glanze. *Pearls of Wisdom*. New York: Harper and Row, 1987.

Airola, Paavo. *How to Keep Slim, Healthy and Young with Juice Fasting*. Phoenix, AZ: Health Plus, 1971.

Auden, W.H. and Louis Kronenberger. *The Viking Book of Aphorisms*. New York: Penguin Books, 1981.

Bach, Edward. *Heal Thyself*. Essex, England: C.W. Daniel Company, 1931.

Barrows, Marjorie. *1000 Beautiful Things*. New York: Spencer Press, 1957.

Bartlett, John. *Familiar Quotations*, 14th Edition. Boston: Little, Brown and Company, 1968.

Bauman, Edward and Armand Ian Brint, Lorin Piper and Amelia Wright. *The Holistic Health Lifebook*. Berkeley, CA: And/Or Press, 1981.

Berman, Phillip L. *The Courage of Conviction*. New York: Ballantine Books, 1985.

Bloch, Douglas. *Words That Heal*. Portland, OR: Pallas Communications, 1988.

Bohle, Bruce. *The Home Book of American Quotations*. New York: Dodd, Mead and Co., 1967.

Borysenko, Joan. *Minding the Body, Mending the Mind*. Reading, MA: Addison-Wesley Publishing Co., 1987.

Bradshaw, John. *Bradshaw On: The Family*. Deerfield Beach, FL: Health Communications, 1988.

Bragg, Paul C. and Patricia Bragg. *Toxicless Diet*. Santa Barbara, CA: Health Science, 1985.

Brussell, Eugene E. *Dictionary of Quotable Definitions*. Englewood Cliffs, NJ: Prentice-Hall, 1970.

Buscaglia, Leo. *Living, Loving and Learning*. Thorofare, NJ: Slack, Inc., 1982.

Buscaglia, Leo. *Bus 9 to Paradise*. Thorofare, NJ: Slack, Inc., 1986.

Carlson, Richard and Benjamin Shield. *Healers on Healing*. Los Angeles: Jeremy P. Tarcher, 1989.

Casey, Karen and Martha Vanceburg. *The Promise of a New Day*. Minneapolis, MN: Winston Press and Co., 1983.

Cohen, J.M. and M.J. Cohen. *The Penguin Dictionary of Modern Quotations*, 2nd Edition. New York: Penguin Books, 1981.

Collison, Robert and Mary Collison. *Dictionary of Foreign Quotations*. New York: Facts on File, 1980.

Cooper, Kenneth H. *The Aerobics Way*. New York: M. Evans and Co., 1977.

Cooper, Kenneth H. *Running Without Fear*. New York: M. Evans and Co., 1985.

Cott, Alan. *Fasting as a Way of Life*. New York: Bantam Books, 1977.

Coudert, Jo. *Advice From a Failure*. New York: Stein and Day, 1965.

Cousins, Norman. *Human Options*. New York: W.W. Norton and Co, 1981.

Dean, Amy E. *Night Light*. Center City, MN: Hazeldon, 1986.

Diamond, Harvey and Marilyn Diamond. *Living Health*. New York: Warner Books, 1987.

Dirksen, Everett McKinley and Herbert V. Prochnow. *Quotation Finder*. New York: Harper and Row, 1971.

Edwards, Tryon. *The New Dictionary of Thoughts*. USA: Standard Book Co., 1966.

Eisel, Deborah Davis and Jill Swanson Reddig. *Dictionary of Contemporary Quotations*. USA: John Gordon Burke Publisher, Inc., 1981.

Evans, Bergen. *Dictionary of Quotations*. New York: Delacorte Press, 1968.

Fixx, Jim. *Jim Fixx's Second Book of Running*. New York: Random House, 1978.

Gawain, Shakti. *Reflections in the Light*. Compiled by Denise Grimshaw. San Rafael, CA: New World Library, 1988.

Green, Jonathon. *Morrow's International Dictionary of Contemporary Quotations*. New York: William Morrow and Company, 1982.

Gross, John. *The Oxford Book of Aphorisms*. Oxford, England: Oxford University Press, 1983.

Hay, Louise L. *You Can Heal Your Life*. Santa Monica, CA: Hay House, 1987.

Hittleman, Richard. *Richard Hittleman's 30 Day Yoga Meditation Plan*. New York: Bantam Books, 1978.

Hubbard, Elbert. *Elbert Hubbard's Scrap Book*. New York: William H. Wise and Co., 1923.

Jensen, Bernard. *World Keys to Health and Long Life*. Provo, UT: Bi World Publishers, 1975.

Katz, Marjorie P. and Jean S. Arbeiter. *Pegs to Hang Ideas On*. New York: M. Evans and Co., 1973.

Kin, David. *Dictionary of American Maxims*. New York: Philosophical Library, 1955.

Krishnamurti, J. *Think on These Things*. New York: Harper and Row, 1964.

Kübler-Ross, Elisabeth. *On Death and Dying*. New York: MacMillan Publishing Co., 1969.

Kübler-Ross, Elisabeth. *Death: The Final Stage of Growth*. Englewood Cliffs, NJ: Prentice-Hall, Inc., 1975.

Latham, Edward. *Famous Sayings and Their Authors*. Detroit, MI: Gale Research Co., 1970.

LeShan, Lawrence. *How to Meditate*. Boston: Little, Brown and Co., 1974.

Locke, Steven and Douglas Colligan. *The Healer Within*. New York: New American Library, 1986.

McWilliams, Peter and John-Roger. *You Can't Afford the Luxury of a Negative Thought*. Los Angeles: Prelude Press, 1989.

One Day at a Time in Al-Anon. New York: Al-Anon Family Group Headquarters, 1987.

Partnow, Elaine. *Quotable Woman 1800–1981*. New York: Facts on File, 1982.

Partnow, Elaine. *The Quotable Woman From Eve to 1799*. New York: Facts on File, 1985.

Pitzele, Sefra Kobrin. *One More Day*. New York: Harper/ Hazelden, 1988.

Pool, Mary Jane and Caroline Seebohm. *The House and Garden Book of Total Health*. New York: G.P. Putnam's Sons, 1974.